T0356513

IT HAPPENED IN
YELLOWSTONE

IT HAPPENED IN
YELLOWSTONE

Stories of Events and People that
Shaped **AMERICA'S FIRST NATIONAL PARK**

Third Edition

ERIN H. TURNER

Globe
Pequot

ESSEX, CT

Globe Pequot

An imprint of The Globe Pequot Publishing Group, Inc.
64 South Main Street
Essex, CT 06426
www.globepequot.com

Distributed by NATIONAL BOOK NETWORK

Copyright © 2025 by The Globe Pequot Publishing Group, Inc.
Illustrations by Kathi Ha

All rights reserved. No part of this book may be reproduced in any form or by any electronic or mechanical means, including information storage and retrieval systems, without written permission from the publisher, except by a reviewer who may quote passages in a review.

British Library Cataloguing in Publication Information available

Library of Congress Cataloging-in-Publication Data
Names: Turner, Erin H., 1973– author.
Title: It happened in Yellowstone : stories of events and people that shaped America's first national park / Erin H. Turner.
Description: Third edition. | Essex, CT : Globe Pequot, [2025] | Series: It happened in series | Includes bibliographical references and index.
Identifiers: LCCN 2024048423 (print) | LCCN 2024048424 (ebook) | ISBN 9781493088560 (paperback) | ISBN 9781493088577 (ebook)
Subjects: LCSH: Yellowstone National Park—History—Anecdotes.
Classification: LCC F722 .T87 2025 (print) | LCC F722 (ebook) | DDC 978.7/52—dc23/eng/20241211
LC record available at https://lccn.loc.gov/2024048423
LC ebook record available at https://lccn.loc.gov/2024048424

♾️™ The paper used in this publication meets the minimum requirements of American National Standard for Information Sciences—Permanence of Paper for Printed Library Materials, ANSI/NISO Z39.48-1992.

The publisher gratefully acknowledges the assistance of the Yellowstone Association, Yellowstone National Park.

CONTENTS

PREFACE

When tourism started in Yellowstone, shortly after its designation as the world's first national park in March 1872, visitors called it "Wonderland." To me it is still a wonderland—and I still get goose bumps when I cross through the Roosevelt Arch and with the first elk I see as I enter Mammoth Hot Springs.

It's hard to narrow down the history of a place that means so much to so many people into twenty-nine or so episodes that enlighten and entertain—everyone has their own Yellowstone story. With all of the firsts, greatest, biggest, and bests of "Wonderland," the author who starts to tell the stories is almost faced with too much information and too much emotion.

To tell all of Yellowstone's history is a task that has been ably attempted by other authors. This book is an attempt to tell some of the big stories but it is also an effort to tell some of the little stories from one of the world's biggest and most magnificent natural places. From the story of a woman taken hostage by the Nez Perce during their historic flight from the

U.S. Army to the tale of the first bicycle trip through the park to the account of a little boy's pranks on early visitors, these stories are meant to be especially accessible and enjoyable for younger readers. I hope that this book is used for projects and reports on Yellowstone by schoolchildren and that their parents will enjoy it with them—influencing them perhaps to take their own children to a wonderland that isn't graced by plastic castles and larger-than-life mice. Each story in this book is complete, and the chapters may be read out of sequence.

I was fortunate as a thirteen-year-old girl to have been taken to Yellowstone National Park by my parents with my brother and sister next to me in the back seats of the minivan. We pressed our noses to the windows, searching the forests for bears and other wildlife. Bison roamed at the roadside and blocked our path to the restrooms—though we had seen them near our Kansas home, there was something more exciting about their presence in Yellowstone. We sat with our feet in cold mountain streams and explored the geyser basins and forests together—before the 1988 fires made for a landscape that always made me think of the gray stubble on the faces of old men before the new green growth of the lodgepole pines filled the landscape with color again.

I also feel especially fortunate that for nearly thirty years, I lived less than three hours from the entrance to Yellowstone National Park, within easy reach for weekend excursions and opportunities to get to know it better. My husband and I now forget how many times we've been there or on what trip we saw what—but whenever we are in the park, we tell each other the stories of the last time or that time that we were here or there. We mark the passing of time by the growth of the trees that have sprung from the ground in the aftermath of those fires—and feel lucky that we were both fortunate enough to see the landscape before and after that watershed. And we've now introduced our two daughters to the wonders of Wonderland, from hikes near the Bechler Ranger Station in the far southwest corner of the park to hours spent watching mother grizzlies and their young from the road in early spring to visions of double rainbows rising over the mountains as we've driven in from the West Yellowstone entrance. They marvel at the little trees and don't even realize how much fire has shaped the landscape.

So, I'd like to thank my parents and brother and sister for that first trip and also my husband, Ross—who proposed to me on the shore of Riddle Lake—for the many subsequent ones that have helped me know the park and him—and now our daughters—better. We all sat together beneath the Roosevelt Arch in 2016 to hear John Prine and Emmylou Harris perform at the centennial anniversary of the National Park Service, making another spectacular Yellowstone memory.

600,000 YEARS AGO

The Making of Wonderland

All across the earth, mountains grew by millimeters and centimeters over millions and millions of years and were then just as slowly ground down by rain, ice, and wind. Glaciers crept back and forth across the planet's surface, carving valleys, dropping boulders and rocks, and spreading soil. The chunks of the earth's crust that floated like giant plates over molten liquid underneath, forming major landmasses and continents, inched toward each other at an infinitesimal crawl.

Then, about 600,000 years ago, the land just south of the 45th parallel of latitude in the Northern Hemisphere in what is now far northwestern Wyoming bulged upward like a rising lump of dough, building with a tremendous pressure, and then blew its top off, spewing tons of ash and molten rock.

Yellowstone National Park sits on top of the land where this explosion created one of the world's largest calderas, or volcanic craters, over what is informally referred to as a hot spot on the earth's crust. The many pieces of hard-rock crust that make up the earth's surface float on top of what is referred to as the earth's mantle, which is made up of a molten rock that is called magma when in its liquid state under the earth's surface. Once out of the earth's protective confines, people call this molten rock "lava," the fiery-hot liquid that pours out of volcanoes.

In most places, the earth's crust is so thick that from above the hot magma under the surface doesn't seem to affect the crust, but in Yellowstone, there is a chamber of hot, molten rock just a few miles under the surface that has some extraordinary effects aboveground. Cracks in the earth's crust allow water from lakes, rivers, rain, and melting snow to find its way under the surface to then be heated by the hot rock. Visitors to Yellowstone know that heated water ends up at the surface either as a placid, lovely hot spring, a gurgling mudpot, a steaming fumarole, or a high-spouting geyser.

People have been studying Yellowstone's thermal features for many years, and though they can describe their actions, they cannot always predict when they will be active or whether they'll evolve from one kind to another. They do know that the four basic types of thermal features have one thing in common—hot water. A hot spring is a place where the superheated water from beneath the surface of the earth rises to the top but doesn't explode into the air because it is able to cool quickly enough to keep it from bursting upward with a fit of energy. Hot springs can be still, deep pools or have flowing water like the springs at Mammoth Hot Springs. The mineral content of the soil around the water, the heat of the water, and the algae found in it determine the color and shape of the features.

Geysers are hot springs that have a more constricted opening, so the superheated water doesn't cool quickly as it reaches the surface of the earth. When the water of the geyser becomes hot enough, it increases the pressure in the geyser to the point where it has to be released in an explosion of water and steam through the geyser's mouth, or cone. Mudpots have plumbing like geysers and hot springs, but the highly acidic water found in these features rises through clay soil at the surface, dissolving it into a gurgling mess of mud that boils and spits. Fumaroles are located where there is a little water—not as much as there is at a geyser or hot spring—that makes its way down into the cracks and fissures of the earth to be heated. Therefore, only steam is released—sometimes with a powerful roar—when the pressure of the hot underground steam builds up.

Scientists don't know why the Yellowstone area in particular is such a hot spot, but they do believe that for whatever reason, the hot molten rock under Yellowstone became superheated and melted part of the crust. The heated magma swelled tremendously and pushed the crust of the earth up into a dome. Eventually, the pressure on the stretched crust grew too great, and the chamber exploded. This explosion 600,000 years ago spread ash all over what is now the western United States—even as far east as Iowa. And when the land shrunk back into the space left by the explosion, it formed the caldera, a bowl-shaped impression in the earth. The Yellowstone Caldera is enormous—around forty miles across—and it forms a significant portion of the Yellowstone area. Visitors drive over the edge of the caldera all the time without noticing—but they do notice the spectacular hot-water displays put on by the park's thermal features, the stars of what early visitors called Wonderland.

1800

The Change of the Seasons

The autumn wind blew cold at night, and the elk had begun their forlorn bugling, sending up trails of steam into the air with their wild, whistling cries. Deep drifts of snow would soon blanket the ground, and then the bighorn sheep would begin their annual battles for mates on the rocky cliffsides, the clash of their horns echoing in the still, thin air.

It was time for the Sheepeater families to head to winter camp, where they could spend a more comfortable season with the other Sheepeaters, pooling their resources from the more bountiful summer season. The Sheepeaters were perhaps the only full-time human residents of Yellowstone National Park until it was discovered by white trappers and its wonders were eventually opened to the world. They subsisted mainly by hunting the bighorn sheep that lived in what is now the Yellowstone area, as well as elk, deer, fish, and other smaller animals. The time for gathering berries and herbs—another main part of the Sheepeater diet—was over for another year, and now they would travel on foot from their upland summer homes, with their large dogs pulling travois, heading to a lower elevation. Their dogs were important to the Sheepeaters, as they did not have horses like many surrounding tribes did.

By the late eighteenth century, horses had become an important part of many native cultures on the Great Plains, having been introduced onto the North American continent by Spanish explorers who were busy colonizing South America. Early in the nineteenth century, most of the other Shoshone tribal groups—of which the Sheepeaters were just one—had acquired horses and guns, which had also been introduced by the Spanish. But for whatever reason, the Sheepeaters had not taken up the ways of many of their Great Plains relatives, and they were forced into harsher, less desirable land within the traditional range of the Shoshone for their own survival. The land at the headwaters of the Yellowstone River, with its rugged terrain and long, cold winters, was excellent habitat for the bighorn sheep and other game, so with plentiful resources available, it became the Sheepeaters' home.

All around the Shoshone land, and around the Sheepeaters in their small, hidden corner, Native American culture was evolving rapidly with the use of the horse and gun. Great bands traveled together to hunt buffalo, and the skin-covered teepee evolved as the mobile shelter of choice all along the Great Plains. Sheepeaters generally lived in small family groups for most of the year because hunting the bighorn sheep they depended on was simpler with a smaller group. The Sheepeaters didn't live in grand, painted teepees but rather in low structures constructed of brush covered with grass mats—and these were usually built against the face of a cliff or under an overhang in order to preserve as much heat as possible from their fires.

Though the Sheepeaters were the only full-time residents of Yellowstone, evidence shows that early peoples began traveling through the area for hunting and fishing as much as ten thousand years ago. And during the Sheepeaters' residence there in the years after the introduction of the gun and horse, other tribes continued to use the area. The Bannock, in particular, who coexisted fairly peacefully with the Shoshones, used a route that has come to be known as the Bannock Trail, which began in Idaho and crossed the Gallatin Mountains before turning south into Yellowstone, passing Mammoth Hot Springs, and continuing west across the bison-rich Lamar Valley. The Flathead Indians to the north and the Nez Perce to the northeast also used the trail for the hunting of buffalo. In fact, the teepee-shaped stick structures found in Yellowstone National Park that were once identified by archaeologists as Sheepeater wickiups were probably temporary shelters erected and used by Crow Indians on brief trips into the high Yellowstone country.

Early hunting and trapping parties of white men encountered the Bannocks, Flatheads, and Nez Perce as they explored the region of the Yellowstone River, and they heard from those native peoples fantastic stories of the geothermal wonders to be found within the circle formed by the high mountain peaks. It was from these early white trappers that the Sheepeaters got their name, and Sheepeater Cliff near Mammoth Hot Springs recognizes their long presence in the area.

But for all of their long residence and success in eking out an existence in this cold, harsh climate, the United States government never recognized any claim that the Sheepeaters had to the land where they hunted and gathered and raised their families. In 1871, just before the creation of the world's first national park in their homeland, the remaining Sheepeaters were moved onto the Wind River Reservation in Wyoming, where they were forced to give up their primitive mountain lifestyle.

1829

Joe Meek's Escape

The party of trappers made its way up the Madison River Valley from the Teton Valley in Idaho easily and with great anticipation. This mountainous land did indeed seem like it would be rich with beaver and other fur-bearing game—and that's just what they were here to get. They could easily make their fortunes here and have a grand adventure in a short time, they thought.

For years, ever since the Lewis and Clark Expedition made its legendary journey west to the Pacific Ocean, trappers had been filtering into the northern Rocky Mountains in search of the valuable furs that were in great demand in the East, particularly the beaver pelt that was prized for its use in fashionable hats for men. But more and more, stories of a fantastic region of hot water and steam were reaching the ears of the trappers who ventured into the fertile river valleys at the headwaters of the Missouri River, and their curiosity about the area was heightened.

But the hapless group of trappers making their way north up the Madison River Valley wasn't doing so to see the wonders of Yellowstone. Instead, they faced a common danger of those early days—an encounter with unfriendly Blackfeet Indians. The party was probably attacked at an area that is now known as the Devil's Slide. Two trappers were killed and supplies and horses scattered as the others rushed toward safety.

Nineteen-year-old Joe Meek, fresh in from St. Louis, Missouri, was one of the lucky escapees. He managed to flee with his gun, a blanket, and a pack mule. For four days he moved south, hoping to come across the other trappers—who were nowhere to be seen—and then he ascended a small mountain. Beyond it was a sight unlike any he'd ever seen.

Meek later said of the place he stumbled upon, "The whole country beyond was smoking with the vapor from boiling springs, and burning with gasses issuing from small craters, each of which was emitting a sharp whistling sound." Some of these features, he said, were immense—four to six miles across even—and others had bursts of blue flame and molten brimstone to recommend them.

Meek must have been traumatized by the events leading up to his discovery of the area. That fact, combined with what was known as the trapper's tendency to improve a story by exaggeration, must have made for lurid descriptions when he rejoined his fur company after two older trappers sent out by Captain William Sublette eventually found the young man and transported him to the permanent fort of the American Fur Company. Meek shared his stories with his companions at the fort, which was being built at the headwaters of the Missouri River.

Over the next few years, many trappers made their way into the geothermal regions of what is now Yellowstone National Park, and even Joe Meek returned with his brother in 1831. Slowly, through the wild tales spread by the campfire, Yellowstone gained a reputation for the wonders that would propel it into becoming the first national park, and though the stories were often exaggerated, no one who saw its wonders for themselves could be disappointed by the reality.

1866

It Didn't Happen in Yellowstone

Jim Bridger had a reputation as a liar, and his friends were only too happy to spread that reputation in the tales that they told and retold and shared with still more folks whenever the opportunity arose. Bridger was surely an entertaining story-teller, and his tales were sure fun to spread to the tenderfoots who came around asking about the mysterious region along the Yellowstone River.

Bridger probably knew the Yellowstone region better than anyone else in the 1860s, when he became famous for his tall tales. Many of the stories attributed to Bridger were probably told by other people, but his reputation made him an easy person on whom to blame any wild tale—and he went along for the ride, willing to share in the fun.

Bridger had come west to be a fur trapper as a young man, and when the trapping trade ended in the 1840s with the depletion of the beaver in the western rivers, he opened a way station on the Oregon Trail and worked as a guide for hunting parties and emigrants, a likely audience for his wild stories. In the 1860s, Bridger worked as a scout for the U.S. Army.

He seemed to take immediately to the kind of tall tales that trappers shared with each other around their campfires at night for entertainment and that they used on eastern "dudes" when they wanted a little fun. Soon Bridger was given credit for being the biggest liar around, for spreading fantastic stories about the high plateau of land around the Yellowstone that only Native Americans and a few white trappers had seen.

But it seemed more and more that there might be a kernel of truth in Bridger's tales. Nathaniel P. Langford, a dude from the east who had come west due to the news of gold strikes and who would become the first superintendent of the first national park, once said that Bridger told him a tale about the valley of the Yellowstone River:

> I first became acquainted with Bridger in the year 1866. . . . He told me in Virginia City, Mont., at that time, of the existence of hot spouting springs in the vicinity of the source of the Yellowstone and Madison Rivers, and said that he had seen a column of water as large as his body, spout as high as the flag pole in Virginia City, which was about sixty (60) feet high. The more I pondered upon this statement, the more I was impressed with the probability of its truth.

By the time Langford heard Bridger's tale of the geyser, the stories that had come out of the valley of the Yellowstone as told by trappers were becoming well known to visitors of that region. Some of the stories were almost real enough to be believable, but no one had yet seen the whole of the park to lend credibility to the tales, and the overblown stories told by trappers made the whole thing seem more and more ridiculous.

All of these stories may have started with tales spread by friends of John Colter, a member of the Lewis and Clark Expedition from 1803 to 1806. Colter remained in the West to make his living as a trapper after the expedition, and stories began circulating that he had discovered a spot where water boiled up from the ground. Around the end of the nineteenth century, after Yellowstone gained its reputation as a land of geysers, some people associated Colter's discovery with Yellowstone, and even nicknamed it "Colter's Hell" after the tales that spread of his strange encounter. (Now, most historians believe that the area Colter saw, if he saw anything, was near Cody, Wyoming, not in Yellowstone.)

Other stories that spread about the region—told by trappers—included a strange tale about the petrified tree forest of Yellowstone, where petrified birds were perched on branches and petrified songs still hung in the air. In reality, there are a few petrified, rocklike trees on Specimen Ridge, which fell prey to early tourists and souvenir hunters, but there are no petrified birds or songs like the tall tales claimed.

The tall tales spread and grew to include a story about a stream so fast that the water was heated by friction and tales of an echo with a delay so long that it could be used as an alarm clock. The curiosity of those interested in the region grew just as the tales did, and the old trapper stories caused people to want to explore the unknown land. Soon expedition after expedition would head into the area of the park to see for themselves and come out with their own fantastic stories.

Today, the many legends of Yellowstone are wound up with the stories of the men who first saw it—including Bridger and Colter—and it's difficult to discern what did and did not happen in the days before the true wonders of Yellowstone became known to the world. But we can give some credit to those wild tales for inspiring the early visitors to the park and encouraging them to set it apart for posterity.

1870

Thirty-Seven Days
Alone in Yellowstone

The cold air that would soon bring the deep, blanketing snows of winter chilled Jack Baronett and George Pritchett as they crossed the Blacktail Deer Plateau east of Mammoth Hot Springs on October 6, 1870. Baronett noticed that his dog seemed to be tracking what might be a wounded bear. He later said:

> My dog began to growl, and looking across a small cañon to the mountain side beyond, I saw a black object upon the ground. Yes, sure enough, there was the Bruin. My first impulse was to shoot from where I stood, but as he was going so slowly, I saw I should have no difficulty overtaking him, and crossed over to where he was. When I got near to it I found it was not a bear, and for my life could not tell what it was. It

did not look like an animal that I had ever seen, and it was certainly not a human being. It never occurred to me that it was Everts. I went up close to the object; it was making a low groaning noise, crawling along upon its knees and elbows, and trying to drag itself up the mountain. Then it suddenly occurred to me that it was the object of my search.

When Jack reached the side of the wounded "bear," he had indeed found the man he had come to look for—but Truman Everts was reduced to almost a skeleton and his clothes were worn to rags. By the time that Baronett's dog tracked Everts's painful crawl across the ground, Everts had been lost alone in Yellowstone, without warm clothing, food, or transportation, for thirty-seven days.

To get to this unlikely end, Truman Everts had started out as an unlikely member of the Washburn-Langford-Doane Expedition to the Yellowstone of 1870. A Helena, Montana, resident, he had been interested in Yellowstone for some time and was part of a group that intended to explore the region in 1867. That expedition was derailed when its intended leader, acting Montana Governor Thomas Meagher, drowned in the Missouri River near Fort Benton, Montana. But Everts's interest did not abate; he still intended to see Yellowstone for himself in spite of the potential danger of traveling into an unknown territory.

Everts was a very nearsighted former assayer of internal revenue for Montana Territory, not a frontiersman. On the first day of the Washburn-Langford-Doane Expedition, August 22, 1870, he became ill from eating too many berries along the wayside, and the rest of his party feared that they would have to leave him behind. He recovered quickly though and was able to continue with them along their path to Yellowstone. The rest of the expedition kept a close eye on the novice after that as they entered the mysterious high country.

The expedition thrilled at the sights in Yellowstone of which they had heard so much fact and fiction. The Grand Canyon of the Yellowstone River with its towering falls was massive and more colorful than they could have imagined, and the sulfurous rumblings from under the surface of the earth were even more fantastic and numerous than they had heard they were. The expedition proceeded, enjoying rollicking times at the fire and with only a few mishaps in the way of Lieutenant Doane's sore thumb and Booby the dog's aching feet.

At one point, Everts went on an expedition up a mountain that now bears his name and managed, with his partner, Cornelius Hedges, to make it easily back to camp. His ability that day perhaps inspired false confidence among his companions. On the ninth of September, after another day of exploring, Hedges wrote in his diary, "All in but Everts and we felt well around the fire," and felt only the slightest bit of anxiety, assuming that he would come in as soon as possible.

Everts, however, was in a serious predicament. After he became separated from the rest of his companions in the afternoon, he missed the way to camp because of his nearsightedness and wasn't able to make it back before dark. He passed a relatively comfortable night away from the camp, but upon starting out the next day, his horse was spooked and bolted—taking with it everything Everts had but a knife, the clothes he wore, and a small opera glass. He made a frantic attempt to recover his horse, and when he looked around again, he found himself completely lost. Eventually, he stumbled his way to Heart Lake and the geyser basin there, which was to be his home for more than a week before he stumbled north again seeking his companions.

His companions became concerned when Everts continually failed to return to camp, and they set out to make a thorough search in the snow on September 12. Everts endured a series of near misses and almost-comic close calls as he blindly wandered about looking for those who were looking for him. Finding nothing, Everts's companions decided to abandon the search on September 22 and returned to Helena, intending to send out a fresh team of searchers once they reached their destination.

In the meantime, Everts had been eating only thistles and staying warm by taking shelter at the edges of hot springs, cooking himself a bit when he got too close. He entertained himself by imagining great banquets for himself, but surely he thought that all was lost. When Jack Baronett located him on October 6, he had wasted away to only fifty pounds, he had no shoes, his clothes were barely holding together, and he was dreadfully frostbitten. Baronett carried him to a likely campsite and made a fire and fed him tea with a spoon.

Everts was terribly ill and emaciated, but eventually he was able to describe his adventures to his caretakers and make a full recovery. On November 4, upon his return to Helena, a rare banquet—featuring some of the foods that Everts had fantasized about during his harrowing experience— was held in his honor and in the honor of the Washburn-Langford-Doane Expedition, which had the distinction of recommending that Yellowstone become the world's first national park in order to preserve the wonders within.

1872

The National Park Idea

Things were moving quickly for Nathaniel P. Langford, one of the leaders of a successful 1870 exploration of the Yellowstone region. His party had returned to Montana in the fall of that year full of the wonder and excitement that had accompanied their journey through the magnificent forests and valleys and basins and full of the idea that the Yellowstone region should be set aside as a public park—to be kept free from settlement or commercial exploitation. Letters had been written, support gathered, and, in November 1871, Langford was called to the side of Jay Cooke, the director of the Northern Pacific Railroad, who envisioned the Yellowstone region as a destination for his railroad's passengers. From that moment on, things moved very quickly indeed.

The idea of a park preserve wasn't a new thing in the United States or in the world at that time. From the beginning of civilization, bits of green property had often been set aside for public or private enjoyment in cities and towns all over the world and kept safe from encroaching development. And in 1864, during the Civil War, the Yosemite Valley in California had been set aside as a land grant to the State of California to preserve its magnificent trees and waterfalls in a public park.

In the late 1860s, the rumors about the wonders of Yellowstone had spread throughout the surrounding territories. Several expeditions to the region were mounted in order to catalog its wonders and share the stories with the world. The Folsom-Cook Expedition through the region in 1869 made the recommendation that the park and its wonders be preserved as an unsettled wilderness. Cornelius Hedges may have made a similar proclamation near the base of what is now called National Park Mountain in Yellowstone National Park during the 1870 Washburn-Langford-Doane Expedition.

But it was after Jay Cooke of the Northern Pacific Railroad developed an interest in the area in 1871 that the national park idea swung into national prominence. On December 18, 1871, a bill was introduced in Congress to set aside the Yellowstone region as a permanent national park, "for the benefit and enjoyment of the people."

Yellowstone owes much of its beginning to the legislation that set Yosemite apart as a public preserve for the State of California. That legislation allocated the land for recreational use and preservation for all time—and Yosemite was to be administered under the laws of the State of California, which would be responsible for its improvement and preservation through funds derived by licensing concessionaires. The legislation that made Yellowstone the first national park was nearly identical—though it put the park under the jurisdiction of the secretary of the interior. It also specifically asked for no funds to administer the park, which was one of the reasons that the fiscally conservative Congress agreed to the bill.

In March of the next year, President Grant signed the bill into law—one of the few bills in that era that encountered little opposition in the Civil War–torn Congress. Though there were no appropriations and no plans for management in place to go with the bill, Yellowstone was protected—the first national park. For more than 125 years it has remained, now joined by Yosemite and many others, the cornerstone of the National Park System.

1877

Emma Cowan and
the Nez Perce

So far, the Cowans' trip through Yellowstone National Park had been wonderful. They'd seen the geysers and the paint pots, then climbed into the Grand Canyon of the Yellowstone River. Tonight they should have been in high spirits, planning to break camp and head home the next day with a lifetime full of happy memories and wondrous stories to tell of the sights they'd seen during their summer vacation in "Wonderland." The men pulled out a violin and guitar and began to play and sing while Emma Cowan and her twelve-year-old sister Ida Carpenter clapped and listened, though they didn't feel as merry as they might have. Earlier that day, they had been warned by General Sherman, who was passing through the area, that the Nez Perce Indians had just been in a battle with the U.S. Army at Big Hole, in Idaho, and were thought to be on their way north into Montana, perhaps even passing near the park.

Emma had come to Montana Territory as a ten-year-old with her pioneering family. They lived in Virginia City, and from her childhood Emma remembered the tales told of the Yellowstone area by an old trapper who lived there. Though many people disregarded his fantastic tales of the sights to be seen, Emma was still anxious to visit the area and did so in 1873 for the first time, just after the area was designated as the world's first national park.

The summer of 1877 was a hot and dry one in Montana Territory, and Emma and her husband George required little convincing to close up their house against encroaching mosquitoes for the cooler altitude of Yellowstone when Emma's brother, Frank Carpenter, suggested it. On August 6, the party set out from Radersburg, Montana, with nine people. They were handsomely outfitted with a double-seated carriage, a wagon to carry their supplies, and four saddle horses, including Emma's own pony.

As they headed into the park along the Madison River from the northwest, they heard rumors that there was likely to be trouble in the area from the Nez Perce tribe of Idaho. They disregarded the stories and were quickly so busy enjoying the cool air, beautiful flowers, tasty wildlife, and solitude that they thought nothing more of it until August 23, after they'd explored nearly all of the sites of Yellowstone, when they met with General Sherman's party, which was looking for the Nez Perce.

As they sat by the fire on that same night, enjoying the antics of the men, Emma and her sister didn't know that carefully concealed in the shadows beyond their camp circle was a band of fleeing Nez Perce Indians who had just entered the park in their search for refuge from the pursuing U.S. Army.

The Nez Perce conflict, like so many other conflicts between the United States government and the native peoples of the United States territories, was triggered by an argument about land. For generations, the Nez Perce had peacefully occupied the Wallowa Valley in northeastern Oregon. Since their first encounters with the Lewis and Clark Expedition in 1805, they had prided themselves on never killing a white man.

In 1855, the Nez Perce ceded part of their land to the U.S. government and accepted life on a reservation in their homeland. In 1863, after the discovery of gold in the area, the government asked for more of the Nez Perce's land, and part of the tribe agreed. The other part remained where they were, however, in spite of encroaching settlement by whites, and in 1873, President Ulysses S. Grant signed an executive order that guaranteed the territory to the Nez Perce, invalidating the 1863 treaty. The white settlers continued making trouble, however, and refused to leave their claims. Eventually, in 1875, President Grant rescinded his earlier order under intense pressure. Even after a young Nez Perce leader named Chief Joseph tried to negotiate a settlement with the government the verdict was the same—the Nez Perce were told to vacate the Wallowa by April 1877. The timing would force them to make all of their preparations in the dead of winter and would give them only thirty days to accomplish what in practical terms should have taken up to six months. Many Nez Perce urged Chief Joseph to go to war against the U.S. government so they would not have to leave their homes.

Chief Joseph refused, and as the plans for the move continued, frustration mounted among the Nez Perce. Finally, a small group of renegade Nez Perce went on a raiding party in Chief Joseph's absence and killed more than twenty white men.

When the U.S. Army heard news of the raids, the cavalry was sent in to forcibly escort the Nez Perce to the reservation. By that time, Joseph felt that the use of force was unavoidable, and a battle ensued where the cavalry was severely routed and the Nez Perce began a retreat toward the Bitterroot Valley of southwestern Montana Territory. From there, they formed a plan to go to Canada. On July 11, a reinforced army met them at Clearwater, where after another battle they headed across the mountains, through Lolo Pass, and into Montana Territory. They then turned south, and on August 9, the army made a surprise attack against their camp in the Big Hole. Losses were great on both sides, but again the Nez Perce escaped. This time, they headed toward Yellowstone National Park, and after another altercation on August 20, they found themselves near the Cowans' exploring camp in the Lower Geyser Basin.

Upon awaking on the morning of August 24, Emma found twenty to thirty Nez Perce in the Cowans' camp, demanding supplies. George Cowan refused to allow their looting, and for a while it still seemed that the party of vacationers would be allowed to pack up their belongings and leave the park unmolested. However, not long after the party had moved out, they were required by the Nez Perce to backtrack to a place where they had to abandon their carriage and wagon. They were allowed a few meager possessions, and then their supplies were looted and ransacked. The Nez Perce were extremely well armed, and the Cowans were not since they had used most of their ammunition for hunting during the trip.

Later that day, the Nez Perce forced them to give up their mounts for other barely walking horses, though again they were promised that they could leave peacefully on them. But again the Cowan party was called back to the camp almost as soon as they had left. This time, however, there was to be more trouble. Suddenly shots rang out, and Emma Cowan found herself crouched with her young sister near her husband, who had been shot from his horse. While they cowered there, a Nez Perce roughly grabbed Emma and pulled her aside, pointed his gun at her husband's head, and shot him again. The rest of the party was taken hostage, and George Cowan's body was left where he fell.

After a long night, the party was again given horses and told they could leave. This time, they were allowed to reach the safety of Mammoth Hot Springs, where a grieving Emma was escorted home.

After a week in safety, she heard the unbelievable news that her husband was still alive. Another week later it was confirmed that he would be arriving in Bozeman, Montana, and she rushed there to find that he had made it no farther than the Bottler Ranch, a common stopping place for visitors on the road between Bozeman and the park. She met him there, and though she found him in serious condition, he was anxious and able to travel home with her.

The ending of the story was not as kind to the Nez Perce. After two more battles with the army on their flight to Canada, they were kept in a state of siege in the Bears Paw Mountains in northern Montana as the bitter winds of October blew in. Finally, Chief Joseph surrendered his people with one of the most eloquent speeches in history. It ended,

It is cold and we have no blankets. The little children are freezing to death. . . . I want to have time to look for my children and see how many I can find. Maybe I shall find them among the dead. Hear me, my chiefs. I am tired; my heart is sick and sad. From where the sun now stands, I will fight no more forever.

Emma Cowan later recalled her harrowing experience eloquently as well, with no malice in her heart. She relished the memory of playing, singing, and dancing on carefree nights in the park, and when she looked back on the events that transpired in the following days and weeks, she bore no ill will toward her captors and her husband's would-be murderers. Though her pleasure trip to Yellowstone had been marred, the memory of it did not linger as a nightmare but as a dream of times past and merrymaking. She later said of the Nez Perces taking their horses,

> It occurs to me at this writing, that the above mode of trading is a fair reflection of the lesson taught by the whites. For instance, a tribe of Indians are located on a reservation. Gold is discovered thereon by some prospector. A stampede follows. The strong arm of the government alone prevents the avaricious pale face from possessing himself of the land forthwith. Soon negotiations are pending with as little delay as a few yards of red tape will admit. A treaty is signed, the strip ceded to the government and opened to settlers, and "Lo, the poor Indian" finds himself on a tract a few degrees more arid, a little less desirable than his former home.

But her most eloquent reflection on the Nez Perce incident was this:

> Yet, at this day, knowing something of the circumstances that led to the final outbreak and uprising of these Indians, I wonder that any of us were spared. Truly a quality of mercy was shown us during our captivity that a Christian might emulate, and at a time when they must have hated the very name of the white race.

1883

An Ordinary Journey

It was a grueling pedal to the top of the Continental Divide, and the riders were surely gleeful at the prospect of a long coast into the fabled geyser basins of Yellowstone National Park. Throwing their legs over their handlebars, they fairly flew down the steep, primitive road on their ordinaries—as their bicycles were called. With the huge front wheel balanced only by a tiny one behind, the men hurtling down the hill were in a precarious—and perhaps exhilarating—race.

Suddenly, below them on the road, they noticed a slowly moving mass of Native Americans traveling west through the park. In a time when raiding parties from local tribes confronting tourists was still not unheard of, the men slowed as much as they could with their brakes to discuss their options upon reaching the unknown band. After a hasty discussion, they careened down the hill as before, whooping and hollering.

Such a scattering there was at the bottom of the hill—the Native Americans never knew what had blown by them with the wind. There was no reason that they should have—they'd just been passed by the first bicycle expedition through Yellowstone National Park.

By 1883, the Laramie Bicycle Club of Wyoming had been contemplating the likelihood of a bicycle tour of Yellowstone National Park for quite some time. Most of the members declared that due to rough roads, steep climbs, and unpredictable weather, such a journey would be impossible. The bicycles of the time made the possibility even more unlikely. The front wheel of the "ordinary" was from three to five feet in diameter, and the rider perched precariously at the upper height, well above the tiny back wheel. Each ordinary weighed more than fifty pounds, making the climbs up steep hills, not to mention the Continental Divide, exhausting.

Still, though the majority of the bicycle club thought the trip could not be made, C. S. Greenbaum, W. K. Sinclair, and William O. Owen undertook to make the trip.

So it was that these intrepid souls set out by rail to Ogden, Utah, to attempt the entrance road that then led into the park from Beaver Cañon, Idaho. The park roads were dirt at that time, and the Grand Loop Road that is still the basic route that guides visitors through the park wasn't even close to completion. Still, with their team, guide, and camping gear, the party wasn't to be much different from other groups of visitors to Yellowstone, a place that had received increasing numbers of tourists ever since its establishment as a national park in 1872.

After passing through the thick forests and pushing their wheels up steep hills—and surviving their near encounter with the band of Native Americans and the careening flight down the hill—the party settled in the Lower Geyser Basin to determine their route through the park. At that time, most roads to the scenic wonders started out like bicycle spokes from that location, and many people stayed at Marshall's hotel there, returning to that beginning spot after a day's adventure before heading out on the next.

The first journey that the bicyclists set for themselves was to the Upper Geyser Basin, undoubtedly one of the first stops for many tourists then and now. While there, they claimed to see most of the major geysers erupt. They also recorded their names in pencil on one of the sinter cones, a common habit of early tourists. The silica-filled water that flowed over the cones would cement the writing in place.

The fearless riders visited the Grand Canyon of the Yellowstone and Yellowstone Lake and then set out for Mammoth Hot Springs over "the vilest road a bicycler ever set eyes on." The sandy, steep pitch of the road to the famous terraces received similar accolades from wagon and stagecoach passengers in the years before major road construction began. At Mammoth, the sightseers witnessed another early practice of hot spring and geyser observers. Many tourists would put an object—a boot, a glass bottle, a piece of wood, a picture frame—in the hot springs water and leave it for a day or two, to come back for their souvenir, which would become encrusted with minerals from the water, to take home with them.

The cyclists were justifiably proud of their journey—the first through the park on the two-wheeled conveyances and the first over the Continental Divide—and William Owen had this to say about the trip:

> Some toil and hardship, to be sure, must accompany the undertaking, but what figure do they cut? The shadowy forms of obstacles that were met and turned on this journey arise before me; but all the toil and hardship endured pale and grow dim when compared with the pleasure and the friendship of those whose welcome made our home where night o'ertook us, and left a green spot in our memory that time cannot efface.

As improvements were made in technology, many intrepid cyclists followed in their footsteps, inspired by the same challenges that faced the Laramie trio. The U.S. Army Bicycle Corps toured the park on slightly more modern conveyances in 1896, stopping to admire Mammoth Hot Springs and other famous sites. Though today the road has improved and the obstacles to today's riders on lightweight, specially designed bicycles are such things as frost heaves in the asphalt, bison, and cars rather than migrating tribes, surely the many riders who see Yellowstone National Park from the seat of today's "ordinaries" would agree with William Owen's assessment of this fine way to see Yellowstone National Park.

1883

Lieutenant Kingman's Dream

When Lieutenant Dan Kingman arrived in Yellowstone National Park in 1883, a daunting task lay before him. The world's first national park had been opened to the public more than ten years before, but rough roads, or the complete lack thereof, made travel to the major attractions nearly impossible. Although Nathaniel P. Langford had recommended a figure-eight route through the major points of interest in 1872, by 1882 only 104 miles of the 140 planned had been built, and not very well at that. Dan Kingman's appearance was long awaited and perhaps even overdue.

General Philip Sheridan, famous for his western campaigns, had determined the need for an improved road system in Yellowstone National Park on a visit in 1881 and had enlisted the help of friends in Congress to get money appropriated for the task. The money came through in the fall of 1883, and Kingman, who was with the Army Corps of Engineers, was rushed to the park as quickly as possible. His arrival was late in the year for Yellowstone, though. He didn't have much time to make his survey of the road situation before snow would fill the trails, and skis, not wagons, would be the mode of conveyance.

After Kingman's survey, he knew what his immediate tasks would be: to rebuild the road from the North Entrance to Mammoth Hot Springs and to build a new, less treacherous road from Mammoth to Swan Lake Flat through Golden Gate. The work to create the road from Mammoth through Golden Gate began in late 1883, and the construction crew made it as far as those magnificent hoodoos of the Golden Gate before the heavy storms of January cut off that season's work. After several months of whiling away their time at the saloons of Gardiner, Montana, the crew started work again in the spring and blasted their way farther south, moving whole sections of rock wall and a giant pillar that became an ornament at the southern end of a log roadway that was built out around the side of a cliff. Rudyard Kipling, in an 1889 visit to the park, commented on this feat of engineering:

> We heard the roar of the river, and the road went round a corner. On one side piled rock and shale . . . on the other a sheer drop, and a fool of a noisy river below. . . . Then my stomach departed from me, as it does when you swing, for we left the dirt, which was at least some guarantee of safety, and sailed out round the curve, and up a steep incline, on a plank-road built out from the cliff. The planks were nailed at the

outer edge and did not shift or creak very much—but enough, quite enough. That was the Golden Gate.

Another crew worked on the road north out of Mammoth, far improving the original grade that carried visitors in from Gardiner. With Kingman supervising the plans for expansion, improvement, and repair, the work done in the next two years reduced the cost of carrying freight into the park and lessened the distance that tourists had to travel by thirty miles. Kingman also tried to establish regulations for the size of the wheels that could travel his roads. All but the last met with huge public approval.

Eventually, Dan Kingman was assigned to other work as a part of the Army Corps of Engineers, and successors filled his role in the park, but less successfully. Starting in 1887, though appropriations continued for the work at a bigger rate than ever, the engineers were moving less quickly and the work bogged down. That downtrend came to an end in 1891, when Hiram Chittenden took over the job.

Immediately, there were changes under Chittenden's regime. He later said of his first weeks in the park: "And now my troubles began. Here were practically $150,000 available; very important roads to build, not a sign of a survey or even reconnaissance, or even a passage of anybody over the route to afford us a guide as to where to begin or where to go."

One of the first things he discovered was that a man named Lamartine, one of the work supervisors, was generally regarded in the area as a crook; after a few weeks of watching, he realized the truth in the rumors and fired Lamartine. He was then well underway and went out to work on the roads, only to find later that an earlier misuse of funds was to leave him with a serious shortage of money.

In the spring of 1892, survey crews found that the park's roads were in dreadful condition. In fifteen days, with $1,500, Chittenden managed to get the roads opened, but then he was transferred to Louisville, Kentucky, in the spring of 1893. His superior in Yellowstone, Captain Anderson, called the move "a most serious blow to road building here." The roadbuilding continued under Anderson, but it wasn't until 1899, when Chittenden returned to the park as its acting superintendent, that the roadbuilding was truly underway again.

At the close of 1899, a figure-eight road connecting the major tourist areas of the park was nearly complete, following the plan that Dan Kingman had laid out in the winter of 1883 based on Nathaniel Langford's recommendation. It is still the main road used in the park by the millions of tourists who come every year.

Still more important than the grade of the road or the surface upon it, however, was the building ethic that Dan Kingman brought to the construction of roads in the new national park. This ethic is still applied to roadbuilding today:

> The plan for improvement (of the road system) which I have submitted upon the supposition, and in the earnest hope that it will be preserved as nearly as may be as the hand of nature left it—a source of pleasure to all who visit it, and a source of wealth to none.

1887

Documenting the Park

Frank Jay Haynes was a pioneer in photography when he studied as an apprentice with his sister and her husband in the mid-1870s in Ripon, Wisconsin. At that time, most photography took place in a studio—and with good reason. The equipment required to take early photos was bulky and extremely heavy due to the glass plates on which the images were recorded. But Frank Jay Haynes wasn't content to stay in the studio—he hauled his camera all over Dakota Territory and was himself photographed taking a photo of the Great Falls of the Missouri River in Montana Territory in 1880.

Early on, Frank Jay Haynes signed on for adventure in the world's first national park, taking photographs of its geysers and waterfalls in the first years of the 1880s. The Northern Pacific Railroad, which later had interests in the transportation companies within Yellowstone and had been instrumental in getting the legislation passed that protected it as a national park, hired Haynes as its official photographer in 1885—and he continued in that role until 1905. One of the perks of the job was a special railroad car, rightfully called the Haynes Palace Studio for its luxurious amenities, that ran on the Northern Pacific lines and where the photographer could make negatives and proofs—a difficult task in those early days.

Frank Haynes had been granted in 1884 a franchise to do business in Yellowstone National Park as a photographer, so in addition to the fabulous railroad car, he had his famed studio on the parade grounds at Mammoth Hot Springs, where he created thousands of postcards and stereoscopic views for tourists. These photos, and special images that could be viewed in three dimensions through a stereopticon, made the images of Yellowstone widely known for the first time. But those were summer images of the park, and an exciting opportunity came to Frank Jay Haynes when he was asked to accompany and document a winter expedition through the park led by Lieutenant Frederick Schwatka in January 1887.

Though the expedition departed from Mammoth Hot Springs on its tour in mild January weather, Lieutenant Schwatka's experience as an Arctic adventurer would by the next night seem like a necessary preparation. The party had only made it as far as Indian Creek when they were forced to make camp because of the difficulties of traveling through the snow on their heavy skis, which were controlled by the use of one pole, dragging all of the heavy equipment required for travel and photography with them on toboggans. That night, the temperature fell to thirty-seven degrees below zero, and the next day they were only able to go four miles farther.

Still the party pressed on, determined to make the loop of the park, though on the third day, they abandoned the toboggans and packed as much equipment as they could into their pockets and packs, which meant only a little food would accompany their journey. Luckily, they knew they could stop at the new hotel at Norris Geyser Basin and spend the night with the winter keeper there.

Disaster nearly struck at Norris when Lieutenant Schwatka was forced to abandon the expedition due to a lung ailment and returned to Mammoth Hot Springs. Two of his men stayed on with Haynes, and they were joined by another experienced park explorer. From that point, it became the Haynes expedition, and he took the first winter photographs of Yellowstone on it, though the party nearly expired trying to make it through the heavy snow and cold on a two-hundred-mile trip that took twenty-five days.

One of the results of their near-deadly mission to photograph Yellowstone in winter was a recommendation from the park superintendent that the trip not be attempted by tourists. But the summer trade was certainly successful enough in Yellowstone, and pioneer Haynes made sure he got a part of it. As well as his photography interests, Frank Jay Haynes owned the Monida-Yellowstone Stage Company, which transported tourists into the park through the west entrance. He attempted to join some of the hotel enterprises that were sprouting up all over the park—though the stiff competition and political maneuvering kept a piece of the hotel business out of his grasp. He would remain in the transportation business until the advent of the automobile in the park. However, he had built another important business within the park, as well, starting Haynes picture shops at other popular Yellowstone destinations and consequently shipping thousands of postcards out of the park every year—furthering still more the public exposure to Yellowstone's wonders.

Jack Haynes, the son of Frank Jay Haynes, would be one of the first children to grow up with the world's first national park as his very own backyard. The Haynes Photography Studio, Jack's summer home, sat in the middle of the parade grounds in Mammoth Hot Springs, surrounded by an elk-antler fence. Jack watched the soldiers who patrolled the park as they did their morning parade drills, and he played mischievous tricks on unsuspecting tenderfeet—and he watched as his father made the images of Yellowstone known to the world.

Jack would creep along the trail to Devil's Kitchen behind the party of ladies and gentlemen who were following the Mammoth Hotel porter to the special underground tour of the cavern beneath the terraces. He knew that once the tourists had descended the rickety ladders into the dark hole, he would have his chance for some fun. By lighting just a few slips of paper and dropping them through the slit in the upper reaches of the rock, he could spur the bats in the cave to action and send the ladies screaming.

And with all the time that Jack Haynes spent causing mischief for visitors around his summer home, he also watched and learned from his pioneering father, remaining with the family business in Yellowstone and becoming one of its great documentary historians.

1889

Soldiering in the Park

When the smooth crust on the surface of the snow was just right, the soldiers in Yellowstone National Park could make the trip from Golden Gate to Mammoth Hot Springs in ten minutes—and it was three and one-half miles of breezy bliss. The heavy, long skis that they rode down the hill were the same ones on which they labored about as they patrolled the rest of the park, but to relieve cabin fever and monotony, a flight down the steep incline was just the ticket.

In the earliest days of the national park, there was no plan for management or protection of the wonders within, nor any money to provide for it. At first, the number of visitors to the park was small enough that it seemed almost unnecessary for the federal government to post anyone there for regulation or control, but as the numbers of visitors grew, so did the instances of souvenir hunting and the hunting of larger animals. The magnificent travertine and sinter deposits around the famous thermal features, the fascinating petrified wood specimens, and the animal populations were all suffering from too much hands-on attention from tourists and not enough from the park's supposed protectors.

In August 1886, the U.S. Army moved into Yellowstone National Park ready to protect the wonders within from thievery and vandalism, replacing the former jurisdiction of the state of Wyoming. Most of the soldiers and their superiors probably believed that it was a temporary position, yet another stopgap in a continuing effort to police the park and protect its wonders "for the benefit and enjoyment of the people," as the legislation founding the park had said.

When Yellowstone National Park was set aside as the world's first national park, it was the start of a long series of experiments by the federal government to see how best to manage its new real estate holding. To put it quite simply, the government had never managed land strictly for recreation before and didn't know how to do it.

The first protection and exploration of the park was done by civilian superintendents who lived in the park at least part of the year and were required to work with very little money to provide improvements and protection. The idea was that private concessionaires would have holdings in the park from which they could control the tourist trade and that they would pay a fee to the federal government that would help pay for the need for protection against vandals and poachers. However, the park's first civilian superintendents were unsuccessful at protecting the park from tourists or concessionaires, partly because there was no bite behind their bark. No laws stood to punish those who entered the park and took advantage of its caretakers.

In 1882, ten years after the inception of the park, assistant superintendents were hired to provide policing and protection of the park as well as minimal interpretation for guests. They lived full-time in the park, spending the summers in areas such as Norris Geyser Basin and returning for the cold winter to makeshift shacks in Mammoth Hot Springs. After an 1884 shooting that involved some concessionaire employees, a Wyoming law put the park under the state's jurisdiction. The Wyoming law was eventually repealed, however, and in August 1886, in true western fashion, the cavalry came to the rescue when fifty men under Captain Moses Harris traveled west to set up camp at the base of Mammoth Hot Springs with the unwritten mandate to protect the wonders of Yellowstone—including its wildlife.

Immediately, Captain Harris toured the park with the departing civilian superintendent and detached men to the same makeshift stations that the assistant superintendents had used in places like Norris. By August 21, informal laws were in place to bring order to Yellowstone, and they reflected the wanton behavior of the visitors and locals who had run rampant through the park since its opening. Some of the rules were as follows:

- The cutting of green timber, or the removal or displacement of any mineral deposits or any natural curiosities, is forbidden.
- Hunting or trapping and the discharge of firearms within the limits of the park is prohibited. Fishing is forbidden except with hook and line, and the sale of fish so taken is also disallowed.

- Camping parties will only build fires when actually necessary, and must carefully extinguish them when no longer required.
- The sale of intoxicating liquors, except by hotel proprietors to their guests, for their own use, is strictly prohibited.
- No rocks, sticks, or other obstructions, must be thrown into any of the springs or geysers within the park.

In the summers, when visitors to the park were frequent, the soldiers kept busy policing the park to prevent violation of the rules. If asked, they would sometimes provide their own interpretation of the park's natural phenomena. In the winter, however, they were isolated in the small soldier stations, posted against poachers, without visitors, and unable to travel easily from place to place except on the heavy wooden skis—and downhill was the only way to enjoy them.

Over the years a more permanent camp in Mammoth Hot Springs was established, and then it was replaced in 1891 by the stately Fort Yellowstone, with its sandstone officers' quarters—still part of park headquarters today. The temporary position of the army in the park took on a permanence that would last until the National Park Service was formed under the Department of the Interior, in 1916, and the first park rangers, some of whom were former soldiers, moved into the park. The army left in 1918.

1902

Saving the Buffalo

The three cows and a bull bison made their way south from Cinnabar just north of Yellowstone National Park, to Yellowstone Lake—in wagons. It was the next-to-the-last leg of a strange journey for the animals, which had begun in Goodnight, Texas, on June 21, 1896. The last and strangest bit of travel was on a barge pulled by the steamboat *Zillah*, across Yellowstone Lake to Dot Island, which was to be home to the bison until 1907, part of one small attempt to save the buffalo in Yellowstone National Park.

In the middle of the nineteenth century, more than thirty million bison had roamed the plains and mountains of North America, stretching from the Mississippi River to the West Coast. Before the 1800s, species of bison had even ranged over much of the eastern United States—but encroaching civilization had eliminated them in the east. Nathaniel P. Langford, who would become the first superintendent of Yellowstone National Park in 1872, wrote in an 1862 letter to his family:

> After crossing the Red River of the North, buffaloes abounded everywhere. We thought the herds of 5,000, 10,000 or more, very large herds, until we got beyond the second crossing of the Cheyenne River, where herds increased in size. . . . I well recall the day we camped for the night. The sky was perfectly clear, when we heard a distant rumbling sound, which we thought was thunder but our guide, Pierre Botineau exclaimed, "Buffalo!" and as we could see no sign of them, he said that they were a few miles away. . . . Soon we saw a cloud of dust rising in the east, and the rumbling grew louder and I think it was about half an hour when the front of the herd came fairly into view. The edge of the herd nearest to us was one-half to three-quarters of a mile away. From an observation with our field glasses, we judged the herd to be 5 or 6 (some said 8 or 10) miles wide, and the herd was more than an hour passing us at a gallop. There seemed to be no space unoccupied by buffaloes. They were running by as rapidly as a horse can go at a keen gallop, about 12 miles an hour . . . the whole space, say 5 miles by 12 miles, as far as we could see, was a seemingly solid mass of buffaloes. . . .

Less than twenty years later, the famous herds such as the one Langford saw would nearly have disappeared from North America. Buffalo had always been hunted for hides and meat by pioneers and even more so by Native American tribes who depended on the shaggy beasts for their livelihood. In the 1870s, a combination of a high price for the hides and meats of the bison and the United States government's plan to exterminate herds all across the Great Plains in order to subdue their native hunters, had buffalo hunters coming in on trains to shoot the bison in large quantities, leaving much of the meat and other useful parts to rot on the prairies.

When the herds vanished from the Great Plains due to overhunting in the 1870s, hunters moved north and west, quickly decimating the Montana and Wyoming herds as well. The herd in Yellowstone National Park wasn't protected from the hunters' guns and was in danger as well, but that would change starting in 1883 as the first efforts to protect all game species within the park began. Still, even with soldiers patrolling the park beginning in 1886 and new laws in place in 1894, poaching took a serious toll on Yellowstone's bison population.

In 1889, William Hornaday of the Smithsonian Institution was able to estimate that there were only about eighty-five bison on free range throughout the United States, 200 protected in Yellowstone, 550 near Great Slave Lake in Canada, and 256 on private ranches. By 1901, due to poaching and other problems, the herd in Yellowstone was down to somewhere between twenty and fifty animals. These were the last "wild" bison in Yellowstone National Park.

The tragedy of the loss of the great herds of bison had been felt across the United States, almost before the bones of those shot had been bleached by the sun—and efforts began to rebuild the bison herds on private ranches and in strange places like Dot Island in Yellowstone National Park.

In 1896, E. C. Waters had been given permission to place non-Yellowstone bison and elk on the island in the middle of Yellowstone Lake, intending them to be an attraction for the tourists he ferried across the lake on his steamboat. The bison would live there until 1907, along with a few elk and some bighorn sheep. The effort by E. C. Waters was probably spurred on by a desire to keep tourists on his boat rather than saving the bison—but that wasn't the case all over the park.

A most remarkable effort to preserve the park's bison took place near Mammoth Hot Springs starting in 1902, after earlier attempts to herd the park's remaining bison into a corral in order to protect them failed. An enclosure was built near Mammoth Hot Springs and a herd was purchased from a private ranch. That herd then was interbred with calves that were rounded up from the wild Yellowstone herds in the spring. The captive bison thrived under the close watch of their keepers and were eventually moved to what is now called the Buffalo Ranch, in the Lamar Valley. In the meantime, additional protection for the wild herd had also helped them increase their numbers in the park. By 1915, the herd had more than doubled under the care of their wardens at the Buffalo Ranch.

Today's visitors see bison throughout the park when they visit, winter and summer, and the two-ton animals are awe-inspiring to tourists. Though their presence in the park has caused controversy for more than thirty years because of a disease they carry called brucellosis, which can cause domestic cows to miscarry pregnancies if they are infected by contact with a wild bison, they are still one of the most famous symbols of Yellowstone and of the preservation possible in our national parks.

1902

The Serpent Enters Eden

June 2, 1902, was a pleasant spring day with all of the beauty of towering peaks and new green grasses waiting beyond the entrance to Yellowstone National Park. Mr. Henry Merry and his wife were anxious to begin their tour of the wonders within its borders, so as they approached the North Entrance to the park, he increased his speed to an unheard-of twenty miles per hour, passing the two mounted troops at the gate in a blur—and terrifying their horses. Mr. Merry pulled quickly away from the troopers, who hurried after him as soon as they quieted their mounts, but the distance grew as the much-faster automobile moved toward Mammoth Hot Springs.

Then, as the road bent upward, the car slowed, then came to a halt. The 1897 Winton was no match for the grade of Yellowstone's roads. Mr. Merry and his wife were escorted from the park—after one of the officers posted to guard against the intrusion asked for a ride.

The two troopers who had been stationed at the entrance to the park were there with good reason—to keep the cars out. Most of the transportation through the park at that time was on horseback or in a wagon or stagecoach pulled by horses, and on the already treacherous park roads, spooked horses were a serious safety hazard. The outrageously loud noise that the early cars made was enough to send whole teams running out of control. In addition, those same roads weren't designed for the delicate systems of those cars, as Mr. Merry found out when he came to a dead stop on that first grade.

But though Yellowstone wasn't ready for cars yet, the time when they would enter its gates as the most natural of occupants was not long in coming. Before the advent of the car, people saw Yellowstone National Park from their own wagons; from the seats of large Concord Coaches that were owned by the park's hoteliers, which were in turn the interest of large railroad companies that envisioned the park as a major destination and a reason to sell train tickets; from another concessionaire's wagons; on horseback; or, only occasionally, by foot or bicycle. The trip through the park on the Concord Coach was very expensive. The Wylie Way as it was called—with accommodations in permanent tent camps—was less so but still out of reach for some potential visitors. Early on, people saw the potential of the car for opening up exploration of the United States and its natural wonders to more and more people.

Cars came a long way quickly, and by 1910 most automobiles were safe and reliable enough to make an extended road trip. But road conditions in the United States and certainly within Yellowstone were another story. Most were unimproved dirt roads that proved a hazard to the driver and passenger in the way of ruts and mudholes. However, in 1911, a group of enthusiasts from Minneapolis and St. Paul, Minnesota, arrived safely in their automobiles in Bozeman, Montana, where they left their cars and proceeded into the park on more traditional conveyances. And in 1912, Congress began the steps necessary to provide funding for road improvements to make safe travel through the park by car possible.

Between Mr. Merry's 1902 entrance and 1915, many other travelers attempted to enter the park by automobile, but all were turned away. Safety remained a large concern to park managers. Finally, however, on August 1, 1915, cars were allowed into the park officially for the first time, by order of the secretary of the interior, after tests were conducted that summer to be sure that the improved roads were indeed worthy of their new occupants. The admission rates per car were posted as follows: $5 for single-passenger cars, $7.50 for five-passenger cars, and $10 for seven-passenger cars. Speed limits, which were enforced by noting the arrival times of vehicles at various checkpoints, were not to exceed twenty miles per hour and were specifically twelve miles an hour going uphill, ten going down, and eight around sharp curves. Fifty cars entered the park the first day cars were allowed under those regulations, and the number has only increased since.

Soon after the first cars officially entered the park, the concessionaires motorized as well, and in 1917 buses replaced the wagons and stagecoaches. Now traffic jams around Old Faithful and wildlife sightings are common summer occurrences. The coming of the automobile and the ability to get to and through Yellowstone by car, camping in new campgrounds, and picnicking along the roadsides, has made the park accessible to all at last. And though there is controversy over the effects of the pollution caused by too many cars in the wilderness, some would agree with what Lord James Bryce said of the advent of cars in the park in 1912: "If Adam had known what harm the serpent was going to work, he would have tried to prevent him from finding lodgment in Eden; and if you were to realize what the result of the automobile will be . . . you will keep it out."

1903

For the Benefit and Enjoyment of the People

Several thousand people were gathered in Gardiner, Montana, that afternoon—four special trains had come in from Livingston, fifty-two miles to the north, packed with excited spectators. The formal entrance to Yellowstone National Park was about to be dedicated by none other than United States President Theodore Roosevelt, who had just concluded a two-week tour of the park.

The plans for the entrance included a grand fifty-foot-tall rock archway, and Roosevelt himself troweled the mortar in place for the giant cornerstone to be laid above a collection of articles, photos, and newspapers in a time capsule. The president stood before the crowd after the massive rock was laid in place and gave an impromptu speech to those gathered there. An avid outdoorsman, he extolled the virtues of

Yellowstone and spoke at length about park management policies, and he ended with a hearty, "I like the country but above all I like the men and women," and they rewarded him with loud cheering. The dedication of the entrance had been a huge success among the many huge successes at the first national park. And Roosevelt must have felt that it followed a highly successful vacation.

The president had arrived at Cinnabar, near Yellowstone, in his special railway car, known as the "traveling White House." The train car was a luxurious home away from home, but it would have to wait for his return at the siding just to the east of the northern entrance at Gardiner, since the newly laid track to Gardiner was not yet ready for travel. The cavalry, then charged with the protection and management of the park, loaned him a horse for the eight-mile ride to Fort Yellowstone at Mammoth Hot Springs, which was just to the president's liking. He wanted to see the national park in intimate detail, not from the inside of a luxury train car.

He rode along with Major Pitcher, who was an old friend, and who pointed out to him the antelope wintering in the area and the other animals that were especially of interest to the president, who was well known as a marksman and horseman. The president was to spend the next two weeks on the horse, which had been carefully checked out the night before his departure by a secret service agent to be sure that it was gentle enough for the president—a fact that would likely have infuriated the volatile and robust Roosevelt if he had known about it.

President Roosevelt's vacation plans were to spend two weeks at the junction of the Yellowstone and Lamar Rivers in northeastern Yellowstone National Park with his friend, naturalist John Burroughs. They were to be joined by a detachment of cavalry, and the whole area intended for their camping trip was to be sealed off from the general public and the press so that the president could have a relaxing vacation.

Burroughs, who was well known as an outdoor writer and wildlife enthusiast, was sixty-five years old at the time of his trip into Yellowstone with Roosevelt. He was continually surprised by the attention that Roosevelt lavished on him—and it was obvious that the still-young president greatly admired the older man, whom Roosevelt called Oom John. They both enjoyed their tramps about the area north of Tower Fall together, and Burroughs was especially interested in the birdlife, while Roosevelt thrilled at the sight of elk and bighorn sheep. Once Roosevelt dashed out of camp in the midst of shaving, with his coat unbuttoned and his face in a lather, when he heard that some of the bighorns were cavorting on the cliffs of the canyon near Tower Fall. Another time, on horseback, he rounded up a band of elk and herded them to an area where Burroughs could get a closer look at them.

After about a week of camping in the Lamar Valley near Tower Fall, Roosevelt, Burroughs, and their escorts returned to Fort Yellowstone to ride in sleighs into the interior of the park, heading first to the Norris Geyser Basin. Roosevelt and Burroughs tried skiing, the popular mode of winter conveyance among the soldiers at the park, and toured the famous Upper Geyser Basin. When they returned to Fort Yellowstone on the evening of April 23, it was to a gala dinner attended by some of President Roosevelt's old acquaintances from his previous frontier days and a preparation for the festivities of April 24, when the new official entrance to the park would be dedicated.

At around three o'clock on the 24th, local Masons marched down the streets of Gardiner toward the north entrance to the park followed by the Livingston marching band, and the dedication ceremony began at four o'clock, with the placing of the great cornerstone and Roosevelt's rousing speech.

Although Ulysses S. Grant was the president who signed the order that made Yellowstone a national park in 1872, Roosevelt is the president most associated with it—perhaps due to his love of nature and his obvious enjoyment of the park during his 1903 visit. The fifty-foot-tall arch itself is now known as the Roosevelt Arch. When it was completed later that spring, the inscription—in letters that could be seen from the depot in Gardiner—read, "For the Benefit and Enjoyment of the People," a sentiment with which Roosevelt would have heartily agreed.

1904

A Typical Tour Through Wonderland

In spite of kidnappings by fugitive Native Americans, occasional stagecoach holdups, exorbitant prices, rough roads, and the thick, choking dust, visitors were flocking to Yellowstone National Park. For more than thirty years, since the park was set aside for recreational use with the addition of President Ulysses S. Grant's signature on the first bill designating a piece of property as a national park, visitation had increased. The park concessionaires who ran the hotels, stages, and restaurants throughout its boundaries couldn't have been more pleased.

Yellowstone was set apart as a national park with tourism in mind—continuing from the days when the Northern Pacific Railroad supported its creation with the thought that having such a destination on its lines would fill up train cars.

The Northern Pacific and other railroads owned bits of the concessions throughout the park as well and embarked on vast campaigns to encourage Americans to "see America first" rather than traveling abroad in their leisure time; they also attracted many tourists from Europe. Incited by the stories and images that came out of the park and were printed in the magazines and newspapers of the time, American people came to see their national park and to travel through it on grand tours.

Generally, the visitors arrived at the railroad terminus and were carried into Mammoth Hot Springs early in the afternoon. There, they could explore the terraces and swim in Bath Lake—though ladies were discouraged from doing so in the days before swimming suits were a common part of the traveler's wardrobe. Then they would dine at the magnificent National Hotel, perhaps get the benefit of a veteran hotel employee's expertise about the park, and arise the next morning ready to embark on their journey through Wonderland, as many early tourists called Yellowstone, in either a Concord Coach, Wylie Wagon, or one of Shaw & Powell's coaches.

The Concord Coaches offered the most elegant and comfortable way to see the park. They were owned by the grand hotel companies and catered to the wealthiest of park visitors, who could afford what even they called exorbitant prices. The Wylie Way, as it was called, was a less expensive way to see the park, because the tourists using Wylie Wagons stayed in permanent tent camps—often with many people crowded into one tent—rather than hotels. The third likely way to see the park was as a sagebrusher—the tourist who came in on his own in a wagon or on horseback to see the sites and camp out in more primitive conditions.

The first stop after Mammoth Hot Springs was usually Norris Geyser Basin, where tourists would eat lunch. Often, they bought bottled water along with the crazy tales that their stage drivers told them about the features they saw—convinced that no water in the park could be healthy to drink. The tour of the Norris Geyser Basin would occupy a few hours.

Before 1904, after that lunch stop, park visitors could look forward to another leg of the journey and then a stop at the Fountain Hotel in the Lower Geyser Basin. From there they could explore the Upper Basin over the next couple of days. In 1904, that all changed with the creation of the Old Faithful Inn in the Upper Geyser Basin, architect Robert Reamer's masterpiece, one of the largest log buildings in the world.

The guests who made their way into the towering log lobby of the Old Faithful Inn could look forward to a stay of luxury in the 140-room grand hotel. The powerful searchlight mounted on the roof made nighttime viewings of Old Faithful possible and also helped the hotel personnel point out wildlife in the area.

After the stop at Old Faithful and its grand hotel, if visitors started out with the feeling that nothing could top their experience of geyser viewing at night in the shadow of that comfortable place, Yellowstone Lake and the Grand Canyon of the Yellowstone were still to come. At the lake, boat tours were a possibility, and even a sighting of one of E. C. Waters's buffaloes on Dot Island was likely. The Lake Hotel was another grand old building for the tourists to stay in—and the possibility of seeing bears feeding in the dumps behind the hotel was always exciting. But it was often the peace of the

Lake Hotel stop that appealed to the park visitors after the days of being jostled and bumped along Yellowstone's roads.

Passing the Mud Volcano and heading to the Grand Canyon of the Yellowstone and the Canyon Hotel was the next part of the journey. Whether they stayed in the hotel or in one of the tent camps, legend says that tourists could see a young grizzly chained to the hotel building and listen to the band that played merry tunes throughout the day. They also had the option of peaceful gazing into the canyon or more exciting scrambling on the rocks on Uncle Tom's Trail, guided by Uncle Tom Richardson himself.

The grand tour would end with a left turn toward Larry's Lunch Stop at Norris Junction and a right back toward Mammoth Hot Springs—where tourists could buy postcards and souvenir spoons to show that they had seen all of Yellowstone's wonders before heading home on the train, full of memories of Wonderland.

1908

The Great Stagecoach Robbery

When the crowd of tourists gathered at the Lake Hotel on the night of August 24, 1908, the excited buzz of voices that had begun that morning was yet to quiet to a dull hum. After a brief discussion, the outraged visitors passed the following resolution:

> That whereas the military authorities in charge of the Park have proven themselves incompetent to protect the tourists visiting the Park . . . we urge congress to provide funds with which to thoroughly police the Park and to guard against a simular occurance [sic].

That morning sixteen coaches of the Yellowstone Park Transportation Company had left the Old Faithful area followed by nine wagons and surreys belonging to another park concession company, the Wylie Permanent Camping Company. The groups of visitors who filled the carriages were looking forward to a beautiful day of sightseeing along the park roads. A cavalry officer led the procession, which was spread out over more than a mile along the rough dirt road. The early wagon tours through the park chose to arrange themselves that way because of the large amount of dust the coaches stirred up. The method went a long way toward making the drive more comfortable, because if the wagons were some distance apart, the fine silt stirred up by the wheels of the wagons in front was less likely to choke out the passengers in the other vehicles.

As the first carriages approached a feature called Turtle Rock along Spring Creek, the driver of the first coach spotted a man lingering beside the road. He didn't think anything of it and assumed that the man was just another sightseer. Eight coaches went by Turtle Rock unmolested, and then the man stepped from the side of the road and in front of his first set of victims.

The man had chosen an opportune place to stake out the road for a robbery. His waiting place was hidden from the sight of the approaching wagons and the area was too narrow for the drivers to turn around once they realized what was happening. At half past eight, the robber stepped into the road and stopped the first coach. The trooper who had accompanied the procession to help protect against such marauders was far ahead of the caravan by that time.

The three men perched on the front seat of the coach were quick to move at the terse order, "Get down from there and be damned quick about it," and a brandishing of a Winchester rifle. One young man became the bagman for the robber and had to give up the twenty dollars in his pocket and his watch for the privilege. The robber told the rest of the passengers to put their donations into the sack held by his recruited helper and threatened to kill the young man if the driver attempted to drive off.

The remaining vehicles in the entourage started to pile up along the narrow road as the holdup went on. As the frightened passengers pulled up on the scene, many were able to hide valuables before the lone robber could get to them. As the take from each wagon grew smaller, he continued to threaten and brandish his rifle, terrorizing those whom he suspected of such chicanery.

One woman wanted no part of the potential retribution should any hidden belongings be found on her person. When told to "shell out and be quick about it," she shrieked at her husband in German, "Give him all you got as he might shoot us." To their great surprise, the robber answered in the same language, "Yes, and be damned quick about it."

When the last bosom and stocking had been emptied from the eight Yellowstone Park Transportation Company coaches to the robber's satisfaction, he danced a jig on the side of the road as the surprised passengers watched, craning their necks as they went on their way. Then the robber waited for the Wylie Wagons that he knew were coming close behind the Yellowstone Park Transportation Company coaches.

From the occupants of those wagons he stole—in addition to all of their valuables—two chocolates from a box on the lap of a young woman. He then required another young woman to give up the stick-pin she was wearing though it was only worth nineteen cents. He insisted that he needed it for luck.

In fifty minutes, he had relieved seventeen vehicles carrying 174 passengers of their valuables, though he only netted

$2,094.20 in cash and jewelry. When the cavalry arrived after receiving the alarm from the first wagons to reach safety, nothing was left but a few emptied wallets and papers. The robber was never caught—apparently his good-luck charm worked. He had pulled off the greatest stagecoach robbery in Yellowstone history.

After surviving the robbery and making their way to a lunch stop at the West Thumb area, the stagecoach passengers regaled each other with their tales of near misses. But one man probably summed up the true feelings best in spite of the lofty resolutions passed later that night at the Lake Hotel: "We think we got off cheap and would not sell our experience, if we could, for what it cost us."

1912

Murder in Yellowstone

As spring began to burst over lower and more southerly climes in the United States, bringing spring cleaning and festive sunny days to citizens suffering from the cabin fever of long winter months by warm fires, the six-thousand-foot Yellowstone Plateau was still blanketed with snow, and in Yellowstone's Sylvan Pass Soldier Station, the air was thick with animosity you could almost see hanging in the smoke from the woodstove as it left through the small chimney on the roof. The lonely soldier station was cut off from the rest of the park by the ten-thousand-foot peaks of the Absaroka Range, and no one could see it or knew about the trouble brewing inside.

Five men lived in the soldier station during the winter season, for though few visitors would attempt to reach that part of the park through the deep drifts, the danger of elk and bison poaching was still real enough to justify their presence and protection. Sergeant Clarence Britton was in charge of privates Frank Cunningham, Frank Carroll, and two soldiers who were known as Mutch and May at the Sylvan Pass station.

Winter in the park was bitterly cold and the snow was deep even in March, making the possibility for outside exercise limited, and the options for entertainment inside the cabin were few, particularly since none of the men could bear to look at each other, much less play cards or talk. Sergeant Britton and Private Cunningham seemed to hate each other with particular energy. Cunningham, who had proved he was trouble by going to Cody, Wyoming, in January and filling the Irma Hotel with bullets, refused to follow any orders made by his superior officer. The bitterness inside the little station grew all winter, as the men sniped at each other month after month with no contact with the fort at Mammoth Hot Springs—even though the newly installed phone worked perfectly. The soldiers stopped speaking to each other and to the outside world.

As the end of March approached, Sergeant Britton, perhaps weary of his days with his silent, yet somehow snarling companions, set off on a ski trip—often considered the winter soldier's best relief from monotony. In the preceding weeks, he had felt that all four of the men under his command were starting to plot together against him. A short way from the station, he broke a pole and returned, reluctantly, to the station with the broken ski pole in his hand; he found the privates in deep conversation.

For whatever reason Private Cunningham chose to pick a fight with his disagreeable supervisor. He insisted that

Sergeant Britton put down the ski pole—which Cunningham apparently thought was being brandished in a threatening manner—and Britton shot him in the forehead when the larger man approached him. In the ensuing melee Carroll was also shot through the arm, nearly severing an artery. The quiet in Yellowstone was shattered.

Eventually all four men would be charged in the murder of Private Cunningham, though Britton was acquitted by reason of self-defense. Apparently the court-martial jury thought that Britton's fear that he was being plotted against was valid. The other three were charged and served time for mutiny.

1923

Marguerite Lindsley Comes Home

Marguerite Lindsley was ready to go home. The scent of spring was in the air in Philadelphia, but it just wasn't the same as the cool breezes that blew through the greening valleys and over the sharp-peaked mountains in Wyoming. Her heart yearned for the tender new spring grasses and the soft-looking muzzles of elk calves. So she quit her job and bought a Harley-Davidson motorcycle and sidecar. With a friend from work—both disguised as men—she made her way cross-country to her home in Yellowstone National Park.

It was 1923, and Marguerite had just received her master's degree in bacteriology at the University of Pennsylvania. After graduation, she had joined the staff of a laboratory near Philadelphia. She was one of a very small group of women scientists who were pioneers in the opening of the sciences to women—but she also was part of a much smaller group than that—of people born and raised in Yellowstone National Park.

When Marguerite was born, the management of Yellowstone was still under jurisdiction of the U.S. Cavalry, which was the official protector of the wonders within its borders. The protection of the park was supposed to be a temporary assignment for the cavalry, but it was a great boon for the preservation of Yellowstone. Patrols rounded up poachers and stopped tourists from vandalizing the park's geologic features. As time went on, it became more and more clear that protection was not the only need in the park—interpretation was also necessary.

Stagecoach drivers and hotel porters shared information and misinformation with tourists. Among other wild lies that visitors heard, some guides said that the contents of Fountain Paint Pot were used to paint the buildings at Fort Yellowstone. Other guides even passed along some of the tall tales from old trappers.

With the objective of continuing to protect the park and ending the spread of misinformation, the ranger-naturalist program was born in 1919 when Horace Albright hired the park's first naturalist. Many soldiers who had been on duty in Yellowstone remained in the new program. Among them was Marguerite Lindsley's father, who served as an early superintendent for the new Park Service in Yellowstone and who lived in the park with his family.

Marguerite's mother taught her at home until she was fourteen, but nature was also her teacher. She learned from the seasons and from the world around her, and she also learned to think of herself as special—as someone who could achieve her dreams, even if she was a woman. She wasn't alone in that belief, and others who felt the same way found their way to Yellowstone.

In 1919, Isabel Basset Wasson had become the first woman to be appointed a ranger-naturalist at Yellowstone National Park. Isabel shared the news with her fellow Wellesley alumnae this way: "Next summer I am to be a government ranger in Yellowstone Park. You never heard of a woman ranger? Well, neither have I."

Isabel Wasson's duties at the park were to include giving talks at the hotels and starting a museum. She had been inspired to try for the job after a visit to the park with her parents and thought it a good match for her degree in geology. Isabel Wasson was part of an ever-growing group of women who saw the new profession of naturalist as a great opportunity—and her pioneering was a real step for women. Many women who had studied to become naturalists were serving as professors at women's colleges and publishing handbooks, and now they would have another opportunity to use their educations. Horace Albright, then park superintendent, made the appointment—Isabel was to be the second ranger, and the first female ranger, in Yellowstone. After one summer of teaching in the park, Isabel was hooked—and Horace Albright believed that not only had her story been one of success, but that those of other women to follow would be too.

Marguerite Lindsley would also be named a ranger-naturalist. She was the second female appointee, in 1921, when she was a student at Montana State College. She worked summers at the information office and guided visitors at Mammoth Hot Springs. Then, after her attempt at life in the laboratory in Philadelphia, she returned to the park in the spring of 1923 and was appointed a permanent park ranger in late December.

After her return, Marguerite ran the information office at Mammoth Hot Springs and worked with the park naturalist to develop the park museum. During the winter she wrote articles for *Yellowstone Nature Notes*, a Yellowstone publication, and conducted scientific experiments.

Marguerite also expanded the role of the woman park ranger to include fieldwork—she toured the park reading water gauges in the rivers, inspecting trails, working on fire patrol, counting animals, and observing those animals in their interactions in the wild. Still, the caution that she gave a biographer who was working on the stories of women spoke volumes for the attitudes that plagued the female naturalists: "Do not stress the outdoor world too much—many still think that women's work should be inside and it is a problem sometimes to satisfy everyone even tho I may be qualified for the work in the field."

By 1926, there were four other women on the Yellowstone staff, working as interpreters and police—the same positions as the men naturalists. However, Chief Inspector J. F. Gartland reported to the secretary of the interior that he disapproved of women serving as rangers—instead he urged that they be given some other title though they worked in the same capacity. Even Horace Albright, who publicly applauded the program and tried to reason with Gartland, admitted he did "not like the idea of having a woman on what everyone likes to think of as a 'he man' force. There is a certain romance and glamour to the title 'ranger' which seems to be lost when a woman occupies the position."

The result of the opposition to women rangers was an order from Washington not to hire any more women as ranger-naturalists—and when Herma Alberston Baggley resigned in 1933, the presence of women as park naturalists all but stopped until the 1960s.

Still, the name Marguerite Lindsley was seen as being almost synonymous with Yellowstone National Park. When she died at the age of fifty-one, she was eulogized as the "breath of Yellowstone." And the many articles she had written for *Yellowstone Nature Notes* were compiled in a memorial issue.

She may have eulogized herself perfectly when she said that exciting motorcycle trip home in the spring of 1923 was only the second most thrilling escapade of her life. She always thought that her trip all the way around Yellowstone with another woman on cross-country skis in March 1925 was the greatest.

1927

A Fatal Mistake

Mr. Bauer, the winter keeper at Old Faithful, grew worried when Park Ranger Charles Phillips didn't appear as he usually did around eight o'clock for an evening of listening to the radio and visiting with Mr. Bauer and his wife. The April snows were still deep, but Mr. Bauer set out across the few-hundred-yard walk through deep drifts to see what could possibly be keeping his friend.

As he approached the small ranger station, he could see that the building was dark and could almost feel the cold emanating from the fireless cottage. When he opened the door, he saw that Ranger Phillips was also cold and dead on the kitchen floor.

Just the day before, on April 11, 1927, Mr. Bauer had collected some roots near the water reservoir above the Old

Faithful Inn as he was working to clean out the early spring vegetation that was beginning to grow in the stream that fed the reservoir. He was curious about the roots and took them to Charles Phillips for identification.

Charles Phillips declared that the roots were the camas plant—a common part of the diets of Native Americans in the region, so Mr. Phillips and the Bauers ate them as an unusual after-dinner snack. Mr. Phillips ate two, and the Bauers shared one.

At about two o'clock in the morning, the Bauers were sorry about their bedtime snack. Both of them awoke so sick they couldn't even leave their quarters. Mrs. Bauer, in particular, had convulsions and vomited all night. Mr. Bauer suffered in agony because he couldn't even empty his stomach for relief—and he had trouble breathing.

The next morning, Mr. Bauer went into the chicken coop and shook with chills. Immediately he returned to the house to wait out the agony with his wife, and there they sat until they both had cold sweats in the early afternoon. It must have been those roots they ate, they thought. And when Ranger Phillips failed to appear that night, they worried with reason.

When Mr. Bauer was sufficiently recovered to walk to the ranger station, he learned the awful truth. There, on the floor of the ranger station kitchen, were Ranger Phillips's slippers—right where he had dropped them as he staggered from the bedroom with his shoes unlaced and shirt unbuttoned. As he crawled across the floor in agony, the poison acted quickly—the poison from the water hemlock, which he had mistaken for camas root.

Water hemlock is only one of the poisonous plants in Yellowstone that has the potential to kill—and has done so a likely three times including Ranger Phillips. Water hemlock has the reputation for being the deadliest of poisonous plants because of the terrible symptoms it causes; death camas also can be found in the park, and poisonous mushrooms abound, making the rule of thumb—never eat anything unless you can positively identify it—an excellent one to remember, because even a park ranger can be wrong sometimes.

1959

When the Mountain Fell

Several hundred people were gathered in the recreation hall at the Old Faithful Inn for a talent show when the floor of the enormous log structure bucked under their chairs. The emcee calmly continued his banter as park rangers opened the doors and ushered people quietly outside. Those people at the inn who had already gone to bed also hurried outside—many in pajamas and bare feet. Behind them, the giant logs of the inn creaked and popped.

It was just after 11:30 p.m. on the beautiful starlit night of August 17, 1959, when the quake that struck at Hebgen Lake, just west of Yellowstone National Park, sent tremors racing through the park. While the visitors to the historic Old Faithful Inn huddled outside in their cars, the quake also shook Canyon Village visitors and those at

Mammoth Hot Springs. Park Superintendent Lon Garrison, who had been in bed in Mammoth Hot Springs when the tremors struck, sending chimneys tumbling to the ground, later said:

> We had to evacuate the building [Old Faithful Inn]. Hot water from a broken pipe in the attic was running down the floor of the east wing. Half an hour later the fireplace and chimney crashed through the dining room floor, activating the sprinkler system.... A few hours earlier, with the dining room full, the casualty list would have been gruesome. As it was our only casualty was a woman who sprained her ankle leaping out of bed after the first tremor.

The quake caused a rockslide over the road south of Mammoth Hot Springs at Golden Gate, and telephone and radio contact with the outside world was cut off. The 18,000 visitors in the park that night had no way of knowing what had happened just to the west of the park—nor did they know how they were going to get out or when. Earthquakes weren't unusual in the park. They'd been reported in local newspapers ever since the 1870s—but this one had struck with unheard-of violence.

Thanks to wireless ham radio operators, word of the quake and possible stranded visitors traveled more quickly outside park boundaries. At West Yellowstone, Montana, just to the south and west of the main quake area, a radio operator sent out an alarm at around 11:45 p.m., just minutes after the first shock waves shook his trailer house. Other people in a position to help felt the quake from their beds and hurried to find out as much as they could. Austin Bailey, a road-maintenance worker for the Montana Highway Department who lived at Duck Creek Junction at the southeast end of Hebgen Lake, set out just after the quake to try to clear the road of rocks. He was quickly stopped when he drove over a fifteen-foot-high escarpment between his maintenance shed and the highway. Unhurt, he returned to the shed to call for help but found that his telephone was out. He then loaded his family into the car and headed north, until they finally found a phone that worked forty miles north of West Yellowstone.

Within a few minutes of the first tremors, the news began to spread that the quake had hit Hebgen Lake, just west of Yellowstone National Park, and people immediately started to worry that the concrete Hebgen Lake Dam would give way, flooding a popular camping area with water. Rumors flew that the dam had broken and that the entire town of Ennis, Montana, was under six feet of mud and water. Quickly, rescue operations and survey teams were sent out to find out how bad the damage was. As they headed into the area, they had no idea what they would find and even less idea how many people could have been trapped by the quake.

The earthquake that hit Hebgen Lake at 11:37 p.m. on the night of August 17, 1959, was a 7.5 on the Richter scale—one of the largest ever to hit in the state of Montana—where the quake originated in the Madison River Valley. The tremors shook all of Yellowstone National Park and quite a lot of Montana, Wyoming, and Idaho. Hungry Horse Dam, standing more than 250 miles to the north and west of the quake site, was significantly displaced, and in Seattle, Washington, a floating amphitheater in Lake Washington broke loose from the shore.

At Hebgen Lake itself, the lake bed tilted and sent tidal waves galloping back and forth across its surface for hours. Along the fault lines, the land dropped as much as twenty feet. And ninety million tons of rock and debris broke loose from the north wall of Madison Canyon, filling the valley with debris. The opposite wall received the gift of four hundred feet of the rock piled up at its feet.

When Dr. Ray Bayles and a nurse, Jane Minton, reached Hebgen Lake Dam on the morning of August 18, 1959, a makeshift first-aid clinic—set up in the backs of station wagons, trailers, and on the ground where injured survivors huddled in sleeping bags—greeted them just to the other side of the massive, but cracked, structure. The eerie new shape of the lake and the rocks made for a bizarre amphitheater in which to perform their mission.

Before Dr. Bayles and Jane Minton arrived at the scene, two nurses who had been camped there had treated the injured as best they could. They were among the lucky survivors of the many families who had unfortunately chosen to stay in the highly popular Rock Creek campground that night. The road out of the area had been destroyed in the quake, so survivors were carried out by helicopter.

People parked near the slide had dreadful stories to report of the sounds and sights they experienced when the earthquake hit. But they could do nothing to help the people directly in the path of the onslaught. Twenty-eight people died in the quake and landslide. Nineteen of them were presumed to be buried under the rock.

Today, visitors can still see the effects of the earthquake at Madison Canyon and imagine the night of terror when the earth shook and the mountains moved.

1966

The Family of the Bear

All through the fall of 1966, the scientists watched the five bears, fascinated—they had never seen silvertips behave this way. In fact, for the last year, these grizzlies had acted like no others they'd studied since their project started in 1959. The bear they called Marian, who had two cubs, had struck up a relationship with another mother bear who had only one. The two mothers actually foraged together, their cubs played together, and the five bears—two mothers and three cubs— were even seen bedded down together in the afternoon for a bear nap.

Though sightings of grizzlies were a regular occurrence in Yellowstone and had been since the earliest days of tourism, no one knew much about the giant bears. What they ate, how they passed the winter in their dens, and even why or when they died in the wild was unknown. At that time, one of the only things that most people—visitors to the park and scientists alike—knew about grizzlies was that they were in danger of becoming extinct. When Frank and John Craighead came to Yellowstone National Park in 1959 to start their study of *Ursus arctos horribilis*, the grizzly bear, their plan was to learn as much as anyone could know about the park's most mythical and feared inhabitants and to provide reasons for protecting them. John Craighead later said that their "goal was to find out how grizzlies live, and to use that knowledge so they might continue to live."

Since the early 1800s, when the first explorers, trappers, and hunters began their treks into the western wilderness, grizzly numbers had been declining. From the tens of thousands of grizzlies that had roamed the plains and mountains in the early nineteenth century when they were first identified as a species, only about one thousand were left in the lower forty-eight states by the 1950s. Most lived in Yellowstone National Park and in Glacier National Park in northern Montana.

Twin brothers Frank and John Craighead were both well known as naturalists and wildlife biologists before they started their study of the grizzly. Along with their younger sister, Jean, who became famous as the author of *Julie of the Wolves* and *My Side of the Mountain*, they had spent their childhood exploring the possibilities of nature and had followed their passion for the outdoors into adulthood. Working together, they thought that they could learn what it would take to save the grizzly from extinction.

From their headquarters at Canyon—where a big, old wooden building served as a laboratory—John, Frank, their families, and dozens of research assistants began to watch bears in 1959. One of the great things about their study was the way they were using new technology to track the bears and identify them. For the first time in a wildlife study, they used radio collars that were fitted on captured bears to monitor their movements. By giving each bear an individual signal, they were able to study their habits and movements over months and years rather than in brief sightings at one time.

By 1966, they'd been there eight years and had certainly learned more about grizzlies and technology than they had ever dreamed. Still, their encounter with the bear they called Marian, her cubs, and the family of two that had joined them opened their eyes to yet another world of possibility.

Marian was, in fact, the first bear that had been fitted with a radio collar; the Craigheads named her after the wife of the collar's inventor. Since they had been able to watch her for many years, they were especially surprised when she befriended another bear family. She had certainly never done that before. No bears they'd observed had done that before.

Over the first years of their study, the Craigheads had learned that most grizzlies preferred to be solitary—particularly mothers with young cubs. The mothers were actually very protective of their cubs around other bears; young males especially were considered a danger.

Because the Craigheads could track the bears through their radio collars, they spent a great deal of time that fall watching the unusual relationship that had developed between Marian, her cubs, and the other family. They really wanted to know if the bear families would den together for the winter in hibernation.

As the snow of winter began to encroach on the park, they carefully watched the den sites. Once, they saw all of the bears outside Marian's den, which was an important observation—it proved that adult bears could visit the same den without fighting—and one of their previous assumptions was gone. Another interesting thing about the denning sites Marian and the other mother bear chose was their location. Before their friendship started, the two bears had denned about sixteen miles apart, but in the winter of 1966, they each chose a site halfway between their two former dens.

But the most amazing occurrence was yet to come. In the spring of 1967 when the bears emerged from their dens into the burgeoning spring, Marian, the other mother bear, and the three cubs met again. Marian left the meeting alone. The other mother bear had adopted her cubs.

The Craigheads theorized that Marian's relationship with the other mother had been related to her desire to find a foster mother for her cubs. Nothing less than the survival of the species was at stake when she made that decision. In order to have another set of cubs, Marian would have to wean her current ones. Typically, cubs were with their mothers two years before they were weaned, which meant that more than two years would pass between litters. By finding an adoptive mother for her yearling cubs, Marian was able to promote the growth of her species more quickly by mating again.

Marian and the Craigheads were, in fact, working toward the same purpose—making possible the survival of grizzlies as a species.

One piece of advice that the Craigheads passed on in 1967 was a suggestion to gradually close the famous Yellowstone dumps—where bears had been feeding for years—and to try to help the bears rediscover more natural food sources. The brothers didn't want the dumps to exist forever—they just thought the sudden removal of that food source would encourage the bears to become campground beggars. Their advice was rejected by the Park Service, which wanted to quickly return the park landscape and its wildlife to a more natural state. They intended to end the bears' foraging in the dumps sooner rather than later. The Park Service also forbade the brothers to radio collar any more bears as a part of the same policy.

True to the Craighead brothers' theories, after the dumps were cleaned out during the winter of 1967–1968, many more bears had encounters with humans as they now foraged in campgrounds rather than garbage heaps—making for dangerous situations for both. As more "problem bears" entered the campgrounds in search of food, more had to be killed by the park rangers because they were a threat to humans. At least 160 grizzlies died between 1969 and 1972—many as a result of contact with humans. The Craigheads' most famous bear, Marian, was killed by a park ranger in 1969 when she charged him as she prepared to protect her yearling cub. Marian had ventured into a campground to look for food. No one knew if the grizzly could recover from the losses of those years.

In 1971, the Craigheads ended their study of grizzlies in Yellowstone National Park under duress from the National Park Service, which was making it more and more difficult for them to conduct their research. In more than ten years they had learned more than anyone had ever known about the great grizzlies of Yellowstone, yet their findings failed to influence park policy at first. The knowledge they spread had convinced people that bears were worth protecting, but the methods were under dispute.

In 1975, a panel of scientists under the U.S. Department of the Interior reported that the scientific study done under the leadership of the Craigheads had been accurate and recommended that the Park Service follow the brothers' advice about bear management. It was an important step in the recovery of the species. More studies were initiated following the methods the Craigheads had used, and several organizations formed to help support the recovery of the grizzly population. The brothers' subsequent attempts to inform the public led to the most critical success of all: People stopped asking if the grizzly should be saved and started asking how.

1973

No Fishing Allowed

As people drove their cars across the rustic bridge over the Yellowstone River at its junction with Yellowstone Lake, they could see the shining waters through the openings in the log walkway on either side. Summer visitors had flocked to Yellowstone National Park as they did every year, bringing families in station wagons and their camping and fishing gear—but this year something was different. There was to be no fishing from Fishing Bridge, one of Yellowstone's most famous and popular landmarks.

Since the park's establishment in 1872, policies about hunting and fishing in the park had changed many times. Because of the mandate to protect the park "for the benefit and enjoyment of the people," some managers thought that providing more fishing opportunities would be a way of fulfilling the park's mission. In fact, when the park was created, about 40 percent of its lakes, rivers, and streams had no fish—but park managers wanted to develop more areas for fishing so they stocked many of the lakes.

The desire to increase fish populations in Yellowstone and in other areas developed into a plan to create a fish hatchery in Yellowstone National Park—and over fifty-seven years the trout hatchery near the Lake Hotel produced more than 800 million eggs to supplement the park populations and other trout populations throughout the United States, making sportfishing a big attraction in Yellowstone. The most popular park site for fishing was at the opening of Yellowstone Lake, where the cutthroat spawned in the shallow waters.

From the time it was built in 1902, Fishing Bridge was a favorite of sports anglers who wanted a good catch of Yellowstone's famous cutthroat trout. Summer visitors would see fishermen and women with their lines in the water shoulder to shoulder along the bridge's walkways—which began to have a detrimental effect on fish populations and on animal populations, such as grizzly bears, that depended on the fish as part of their food source.

But overfishing wasn't the only threat to the cutthroat in the mid-1900s; other fish that had been introduced either legally or illegally inhabited the waters—redside shiners, lake chub, longnose dace, and lake trout. The lake trout, especially, damaged the cutthroat population by outcompeting them for food sources and by preying on the smaller fish.

Since 1973, when Fishing Bridge was officially closed to fishing, cutthroat populations have made a fair recovery—but the lake trout continue to be a problem for park managers. The lake trout are extremely difficult to catch because their habitat is generally at the lake bottom (although in recent years their numbers have been reduced through gill-netting programs, as in 2007, when 73,000 of the fish were taken from the lake). Anglers on Yellowstone Lake who do catch them are instructed to take them to a park ranger for identification and by all means not to practice the catch-and-release policy used for other species caught throughout the park. Park managers continue to work on the problem of the lake trout and also chronic problems such as whirling disease, which infects wild trout in rivers outside of the park. But thanks to the fact that fishing is no longer allowed from Fishing Bridge, the park's fisheries and grizzly populations are better protected today than they ever have been, and park management policies will continue to evolve to protect them even more.

—

1988

Let It Burn

Balanced on the roof of the Museum of the National Park Ranger near Norris Geyser Basin, the pair of men worked to hose down the shake-shingled roof while a dozen or so rangers and firefighters gathered near the museum's stone foundation scanned the grayness beyond the geyser basin for the sunset-orange glow of the fire that lurked in the darkness. The firefighters hoped the treeless landscape of sinter cones would be a natural firebreak, and the rangers had already picked out the "safe spots" in the basin should they need to escape the roaring heat. There was no escape from the smoke—no one who had been in Yellowstone that summer had any chance against the lung-filling gray masses that squeezed all of the air out of the air.

The fire approaching the museum that day was part of the North Fork fire, which had started less than two hundred yards outside the park boundary in the Targhee National Forest in Idaho on July 22. But today was August 20—and the fire had been raging unpredictably for a month. The firefighters couldn't be sure of anything as they planned their attack on the encroaching flames.

Still, they stood their ground, hoses aimed at the treetops, while the roaring orange dragon approached and cackled with each exploding tree. And then the two-hundred-foot flames ran out of energy at the very edge of the basin, 150 feet from the museum. But the fire wasn't totally out; a finger raced toward other Norris developments through a stand of trees. But for once the fire had behaved as it was supposed to.

August 20, 1988, the day that the fire headed toward the museum, became known as Black Saturday—the worst single day of fire activity for the whole summer. Winds of thirty to forty miles per hour fanned flames up to two hundred feet high—gusts of more than seventy miles per hour gave frightening indications of the flames' fury. All of the helicopters and airplanes recruited to fight the fire were useless, grounded because of high winds. There was little that firefighters could do but watch the giant orange tongues of flame taste and devour everything in sight.

By the end of the day, 165,000 acres had been added to the ever-growing toll of burned forestland. The North Fork fire had grown more than 50 percent during a twenty-four-hour period, and fires all over the region were growing and rushing through stands of trees. Fires cut off roads and stranded tourists, and emergency evacuations ensued. Surely everyone in the park that day asked, "How much longer can this last?" They couldn't have known that the answer was that there was more than a month to go in the fire season.

Not only were the fires of 1988 long lasting, but they were also long in coming. In the fall of 1987, Yellowstone National Park began to dry out. The expected autumn rains rarely darkened the sky, and snow was light all winter. By June 1988, it was confirmed—the whole Yellowstone region was in an extreme drought. The winds that blew fiercely over the area were warm and foreboding. With the wide expanses of mature forests and few roads to interrupt the relentless march of crimson flames, conditions were prime for a fire, if started, to grow exponentially and be unstoppable.

For seventeen years, the fire policy of the park managers had been simple: Keep an eye on forest fires; don't let them threaten people's lives or structures, but let them burn if they were in the backcountry. Fire is a natural part of the forest system, and not all fires are human caused—though it's important to heed Smokey Bear's warnings about matches and campfires. The first fire in Yellowstone National Park in the summer of 1988 was started by a bolt of lightning that hit some downed trees in the undergrowth of the forest. In June and July, the park managers watched these fires closely, knowing how important they were to the health of a forest because they cleared out dead and dying trees and encouraged plant growth. Still, historic buildings and tourists had to be protected. Unfortunately, fire season in Yellowstone is also its highest visitation season.

One of the early firefighting efforts of the summer was at Grant Village in late July. Poised with Yellowstone Lake at their backs, the firefighters took aim with the steady stream of water from their hoses, ready to retreat into the frigid lake waters for safety at any moment. Their goal was to save the village's buildings from the inferno.

Visitors and seasonal park concessionaire employees were evacuated from Grant Village and other populated areas—but reporters flocked to the scene. Soon public outcry from neighboring communities and from far across the nation against the "let it burn" policy was growing with the speed of the flames.

The gateway communities to the park had dual problems. In addition to the threat posed by the encroaching flames, they had to deal with a dwindling tourist population—which could mean economic ruin in such seasonally dependent communities. Road closures within the park turned many discouraged tourists away—perhaps to return again and perhaps not.

On July 22, a fire was accidentally started in the Targhee National Forest just outside the park boundary. The North Fork fire, as it was called, was one of the worst of the season and couldn't have been worse for the public perception of the fire policy when it threatened the historic Old Faithful Inn. It was the North Fork fire that ended the "let it burn" policy for the summer and caused firefighting efforts to begin in earnest.

But even when the massive effort to quell the fires began, traditional firefighting techniques, such as starting smaller fires to burn off fuel so that a fire would stop, were frequently of no use during the massive firestorm of 1988. The extremely high winds would take embers from the firebreaks and drop them into fuel loads in the forests. Infrared maps were used to track the fires, and water and flame retardant were dropped from above. Still, firefighters on the ground relied on old-fashioned methods and slept in camps to which supplies were brought by horse teams.

With the wild wind blowing, some fires moved as fast as two miles per hour. Some moved five to ten miles in one day, and one actually went fourteen miles in three hours. The result—eventually—was the largest forest-fire-fighting effort ever. The military came in to provide assistance, and helicopters, spotting planes, and aerial tankers were brought into service by the dozen. For a while, Yellowstone looked more like a war zone than a wonderland.

In September gently falling snow made the firefighters shiver as they faced Yellowstone's last hot spots. June was a dim memory, and July and August had come and gone, and still they were working to stop the flames, trying to put out one of the most massive infernos ever seen in one of the most famous places in the world. During the September days when the cold rain and soft snow failed to pelt them from above, the many fires of the summer of 1988 continued to burn, smoldering and coming back to life on dry days as the 5,500 firefighters stepped in to put out the remaining hot spots. But finally, at the end of October, the fires were out. In addition to the 1.3 million acres in the Yellowstone area that had burned, including the more than 900,000 in the park itself, three houses, thirteen mobile homes, ten private cabins, and eighteen cabins owned by the park's concessionaires were burned. The flames didn't end their assault at park borders; more than 400,000 acres of surrounding national forest lands were also burned that hot, hot summer. One firefighter lost his life in a plane crash near Jackson, Wyoming, and $120 million was spent in the effort to put out the flames in Idaho, Montana, and Wyoming.

Once the fire was out, the park service's "let it burn" policy and the hands-off philosophy of the National Park System came under intense scrutiny. Tourists and Yellowstone enthusiasts were disappointed at the thought of the blackened toothpick forests and decreased wildlife habitat. Surely, they thought, it would be better to try to put out smaller fires than fight one like this again.

But with the end of the fires, park managers had nature on their side again. Wildflowers and grasses were quick to reassert their position on the burned forest floors. Some trees, such as the lodgepole pine, have special cones that release their seeds only when the extreme heat of fire is present, and tens of thousands of small seedlings had taken root before the deep snows of winter came. Park managers knew a new, healthy understory wouldn't have been able to grow without the fire to get rid of too much dry, dead undergrowth. Sunshine, rain, and fire are all necessary parts of the forest's healthy life span. The many well-meaning offers of seeds and seedlings by concerned citizenry were turned away by bemused park managers. With their eyes finally clear of smoke, they could already see a new healthy forest growing—a promising start.

1995

The Return of the Wolf

Slowly, the relocation team opened the gate of the pen, moved quickly out of the way—and then they waited. The snow all around them was deep, and the thin, crisp air of March was thickened with their anticipation. The majestic gray wolves that had been gnashing their teeth against the metal of the tall chain-link enclosure since they arrived in Yellowstone National Park stayed inside their pen, far from the gate that had served as the human entrance for two months. Two days later, they were still inside, pacing at the back of the enclosure, distrusting the opening and the people who had brought them there.

In some ways, the crowd gathered around the pen had been waiting for seventy years for this moment. Since the 1930s the howl of the wolf had been silenced not only in

Yellowstone National Park, but also in most of the western United States. Many of the ranchers who were attempting to settle the valleys of Wyoming and Montana believed that the removal of predatory animals was essential to the taming of the frontier and to making ranching a viable option. And to many ranchers, wolves were the most feared of predators.

But it wasn't just fear for the lives of calves with brands that silenced the eerie howls that had once filled the wilderness. At one point, some wildlife managers believed that to restore healthy populations of the more "popular" wild animals—deer, bison, elk, pronghorn—the predators that kept their numbers low would have to be removed from the ecosystem. As a result of both sides' concerns, a bounty was placed on wolves, bringing a handsome price for each thick pelt. By the early 1930s it was believed that the last wolf in Yellowstone National Park had been exterminated, and though the call to bring them back was not long in coming, the science and politics of conservation had to be advanced first.

Yellowstone National Park was itself the product of the earliest conservation efforts in the United States when it was designated the first national park in 1872, but conservationism didn't truly come into vogue in the United States until the late nineteenth and early twentieth centuries. As the numbers of conservationists grew in the early 1900s, so did their knowledge of sound wildlife-management practices, but the road to knowledge was not without bends. One year one theory would prevail, and the next year it would be dismissed.

Opinions about wolves took many, many years to change. The economic interests of ranchers whose livestock could suffer from the wolves' instinctive habits were usually considered more important than the need for the return of a piece of the wilderness, and some people remained unconvinced that wolves were part of a healthy ecosystem. It seemed there was no right answer.

The debate over whether wolves should be brought back into the park raged on in the winter of 1994–1995, when the decision was made to trap wolves in Alberta, Canada, and to bring them to the Yellowstone ecosystem for reintroduction. Helicopter teams flew over the dark Canadian forests and captured wolves that were then equipped with radio collars and released. These wolves would lead the teams to other members of their packs, which would also be captured, and family groups would be brought together to Yellowstone.

Three packs, the Crystal Bench, Rose Creek, and Soda Butte, as they would later be called, composed of fifteen wolves, were brought into Yellowstone National Park and put into acclimation pens. Park personnel picked up elk and deer carcasses off roadways and dragged them into the pens for daily feedings. The wolves were wary of the humans, and every indication was that they would bolt from their pens given the opportunity. That's why the relocation team was astonished when they opened the door and the wolves stayed in.

After two days of waiting for the Crystal Bench pack to leave by way of the gate, the relocation team got another idea. Because the wolves had been so anxious to stay out of the way of the humans when the carcasses were dragged in, maybe they were afraid to go near any opening so clearly associated with humans. A hole cut in the back of the pen and two deer carcasses left outside were sufficient enticement, and soon all three packs were loose in Yellowstone.

Almost as soon as the spring thaw began melting away the winter wonderland of the Lamar Valley, a pack led by a male and female known as number nine and number ten headed north out of the park toward Red Lodge, Montana. Biologists were surprised but assumed that the female was pregnant with pups—the first major success of the program. Most people thought that there wouldn't be any pups in Yellowstone the first year, but the wolves surprised them again.

In April, number nine had eight pups just outside of Red Lodge. If park biologists were ecstatic but worried, ranchers were panicked and vocal. And then the worst happened—number ten was shot with a 9mm rifle by a local who may or may not have even known what he was shooting at.

Number nine was alone with the pups—making their survival unlikely—and the members of the wolf team lost no time in instigating their search for the pups. It was rewarded in late spring, and the pups were "adopted" by the wolf team until they were able to be released back into the wild.

The capture of the pups for their own good would come to be to the good of the researchers, too. As little as they thought the chance was that there would be pups in the park so early, they held out even less hope that they would be able to track and study the first generation of Yellowstone wolves in seventy years as closely as they would now that these eight pups were to be radio-collared and set free.

In the midst of the successes of biologists, two camps were rapidly firing arguments over a bunker of miscommunication and misunderstanding. Tourists who came into the Lamar Valley—many of them day after day during their stays in the park—to watch the wolves in their first steps across those startlingly beautiful valleys of gold, green, and russet couldn't understand the uproar of residents. These were beautiful wild animals finally allowed a chance to be free. How could anyone shoot one of these creatures?

Ranchers and other residents claimed that the wolves would not only decimate cattle populations, but they would also harm the elk and deer populations that attracted tourists. They also threatened that wolves would go after small children—and not even necessarily those wearing red hoods.

Biologists were quick to point out that there was possible overpopulation among the park's ungulate species—that wolves would help keep populations in check. Wolf supporters were hard pressed to change other attitudes about wolves that came right out of Grimm's fairy tales.

But the wolves themselves, by thriving more quickly than anyone had ever thought they would, won the day. By the end of the first year of wolves in the park, some cattle and sheep had been lost, and four wolves had been lost to accidents or had met foul play, but the population was strong at nineteen. When the next Canadian wolves were brought into the pens in early 1996, some of them marched right out the gate as soon as it was opened to take what was rightfully theirs: a place in the Yellowstone ecosystem. At the end of 2023, there were 124 wolves in the park in eleven packs, including six breeding pairs.

2000–?

Steamboat Geyser Erupts—And Erupts Again

The earth rumbled and undulated early in the morning of May 2, 2000, shaking a couple from their makeshift beds in the pickup in which they were camped at the Norris Geyser Basin parking lot. Shaking ground in Yellowstone—in that corner of Wyoming and Montana and Idaho—isn't that unusual. After all, the ground under the area covering the earth's molten core is thinner there than it is most places elsewhere in the world, and the forces that make mountains move are that much closer to where humans have chosen to live and work and play. But earthquakes in and around Yellowstone National Park have had scary consequences, and the couple in the pickup truck gathered themselves and sped away toward Madison Junction before the sun had risen fully on that early spring morning. Five o'clock is typically a quiet time in Yellowstone, at least for the human visitors. A few hardy souls will make their way to the Lamar Valley at that time of day to watch for the early-rising wolf packs and other crepuscular creatures that are stirring, but especially in the quieter early days of travel in May and at that chilly hour of the morning, not many human creatures are abroad. The geyser basins and nearby visitor centers and campgrounds are usually very quiet. Any animals or people who were near Norris that day, though, would have felt the earth shake and heard the roar from the mouth of the cone that was Steamboat Geyser as it opened and began its awe-inspiring display.

Geysers are, of course, fairly commonplace within Yellowstone, so much so that many of the areas designated as must-stops on the Grand Loop Road are geyser, fumarole, hot spring, and mudpot related. Norris Geyser Basin, also home to the Museum of the National Park Ranger, is one of the best areas to stop and enjoy the spectacles made by hot water, farther from the crowds of Old Faithful, diverse in its offerings, and with lovely boardwalks arranged like light-brown ribbons around the best features. One of Norris's most famous attractions is Steamboat Geyser—a tall, dark, handsome, mysterious stranger among the park's geothermal features. The last time it had spewed its steam and water was in 1991.

It must sometimes feel to park rangers in Yellowstone that Old Faithful's reputation has gotten in the way of good science and understanding. Indeed, due to the relative accuracy with which the eruptions of that icon and some of the other regular geothermal features in the park have been predicted for more than one hundred years, neophyte visitors to the park often think that the attractions are, if not available by command, at least easily seen by following a timetable laid out for their use in full color or through a phone app. It's hard to know whether misconceptions about geysers or about wolves and grizzly bears hold the upper hand with the uninitiated.

In the case of geysers, they are surrounded by quite a lot of science but are also tinged with the air of mystery. It's easy to imagine why both early and contemporary visitors to the park—and employees—are enthralled by them. It is an amazing experience to stand on the boardwalk near Old Faithful or Castle Geyser or any of the hundreds of geysers in the park and suddenly hear the noise and see the spectacle of boiling hot water shooting up into the mountain air.

The science is fairly simple to explain. A geyser is formed when a narrow opening in the earth, almost like a straw poked into a glass, allows water to collect near the magma in a hot spot where the earth's crust is thin, like in Yellowstone. The water below the surface, capped off with cooler water at the top, becomes superheated and, as in a teapot that's boiling, pressure builds within that narrow tube. Eventually, the pressure within becomes too great, and the water erupts through the narrow opening out of the surface of the earth, spraying tens or hundreds of feet into the air. Visitors to Yellowstone who venture into the geyser basins see this virtually every day.

But what they don't see every day is a geyser like Steamboat. When Steamboat's steam plume and water finally burst out of the earth on that May morning, it definitely would have surprised any nearby visitors to the park and employees as well. There's no predicting Steamboat.

The last time it had erupted was in 1991, though it had erupted four times in the late 1980s leading up to that display. And it had erupted several times between 1961 and the 1980s. But from 1911 to 1961 it was totally dormant.

But what's most special about Steamboat isn't its rarity of eruption. It's the eruption itself. It is the world's tallest active geyser—throwing water more than three hundred feet in the air during its major eruptions. It's no wonder that the first couple to hear it on the morning of May 2, 2000, thought that it was an earthquake. The power required to push that much water into the air causes an air-shaking roar and vibrates the earth all around it. When a park employee arrived at the geyser basin that morning, the vapor plume was more than five hundred feet tall and the visitors who had fled earlier were back to enjoy the show. More visitors kept appearing, and on May 3 it was reported that there were still eruptions of up to eighty feet of water and that the geyser was also flinging rocks around.

Starting on that early May morning, it became quite active—for Steamboat Geyser—erupting six more times before going quiet again at the end of May 2005. And thus the mystery. Scientists and park employees don't know for sure why Steamboat goes through such long periods of dormancy between eruptions or why sometimes there are clusters of smaller and major eruptions as there were during the first five years of the new millennium. In the years since the last eruption, Yellowstone has been measurably rising above its underground chamber of magma. In 2007 it was reported that since 2004, the swelling of the hot spot had raised the ground three inches a year—more than three times faster than in the past. Steamboat erupting, the earth shifting, the trees growing, the animal populations shifting—all are reminders that in this ancient place nothing is constant.

Another reminder that the very ground changes beneath us all the time started on March 15, 2018. While still not predictable, since that time the world's tallest geyser has been expelling water at a startlingly more frequent pace. Geyser gazers camp in the parking lot, with tarps and protective covers on their windshields to protect from thrown rocks—from the violence of the eruptions—and the heavily silicate waters. Before March 15, 2018, it had been three years, 193 days since a major eruption. Since then, the times between have gone from as few as three days to as many as eighty-nine, keeping the park's visitors rapt with anticipation of the next big one.

2010

Night of the Grizzlies

Snow covered the ground and the air was seasonably cold as a group of twelve preschool-age children watched entranced while Dolly, Loulou, and Koda trundled around their new home at Zoo Montana in Billings on December 17, 2010. It was a pre-holiday treat, a Friday-morning field trip for the youngsters. And though Billings isn't that far from the campground near Yellowstone—only about 125 miles away—that made the cubs famous that summer, it was a great step forward in the story of the lives of the three young bears, offering some closure after the terrifying night of July 27–28, 2010.

The ten-acre Soda Butte Campground, located near Cooke City, Montana, in the Gallatin National Forest, is just outside the boundaries of Yellowstone National Park—and during the record-breaking tourism month of July 2010, it had often seen all of its twenty-seven sites occupied by tents and small trailers, hosting some of the more than three and a half million visitors who would make their way to the park over the year. It's a standard national park campground with fire rings and campsites for tents and trailers, picnic tables, and special containers for food storage. The campground is in the middle of bear country, and visitors and campers are advised to take every precaution to avoid human/bear encounters, which can be deadly for both species.

It was shortly after midnight on July 28, and the campground was peaceful and quiet, all guests tucked into their tents and trailers, sleeping bags and bunks, until some of the area's permanent residents—a mother grizzly and three cubs—made their way into the campground and pulled a forty-eight-year-old man from Michigan from his tent and the screaming started. After killing the man, the bears then targeted another tent, biting a woman on the arm, and then another, injuring a young man who tried to fight off the three-hundred-pound mother bear with a right hook to the nose. It was a terrifying scene, and as the noise awoke other campers, they took to their cars, driving through the campground roads to rescue victims and spread the word that the area wasn't safe.

Yellowstone's visitors have long been warned about the dangers of all wildlife, from the yellow-and-black handouts showing the dangers of approaching bison that accompany the maps and newspapers handed out at the entrances to the hundreds of signs scattered throughout the park reminding visitors and campers that they are in bear country. Visitors are asked not to leave food out or to take it into their tents lest they attract bears. And the visitors at the Soda Butte

Campground had followed those instructions. There was nothing at the site that night or discovered in the investigation that followed that would indicate otherwise.

In the minutes after the mother bear targeted three tents, killing the man from Michigan and severely injuring a woman and another young man, the injured were rushed to the nearest medical facility in Cooke City, Montana. And the family of bears fled the scene.

It had been an unusual attack. Grizzlies are generally shy of humans, especially if they don't associate them with an easy picnic lunch, and the investigators who came in after the event didn't think that these grizzlies had been habituated to human food. Since the 1960s Yellowstone had been working very hard to eliminate the kinds of bear/human interactions that had led to trouble in the past due to feeding and the open dumps. And, according to Montana Fish, Wildlife, and Parks officials, an aggressive attack of the magnitude seen in late July hadn't been experienced in the park since the 1980s, though there had been a similar, but less deadly, episode in the same campground two years earlier. Fear in the surrounding area rose, along with rumors about what might have caused the incident. Some locals thought that perhaps the bear from the 2008 attack hadn't actually been removed from the area, as reported, and that she was responsible for this deadlier encounter. Fish, Wildlife, and Parks employees were quick to discount that as a possibility. Next, rumors arose that a wildlife photographer had perhaps been baiting the bears with food, hoping for closer access.

The pieces of the puzzle would start to be put together when the mother bear and her cubs were captured in culvert traps in the days following the attacks. At first it was reported there were no obvious signs of malnutrition in the bears that might have led to a desperate act. But in the end it was proven that the mother bear had consumed flesh from the victim who was killed, and that the cubs were suffering from malnutrition and clear stress—in July they were still wearing their thick winter coats. The mother bear was euthanized, which is standard policy when a bear shows aggressive behavior and has tasted human flesh.

But the questions began about what to do with the three cubs, which had followed their mother's lead in the attack but were youngsters. In the next chapter of their story, they found themselves at Zoo Montana, where they would spend five months in quarantine from other animals, adjusting to the stresses of life in captivity; learning to trust their human keepers and to scrounge for their food (the keepers bring in food but try to encourage "normal" bear behavior); and playing as siblings. The keepers claimed that Dolly, Loulou, and Koda were demonstrating their personalities, playing just like any other bears behind a zoo enclosure in a way that's safe for the guests of the zoo, and that they were ready for their audience. When the preschool group was able to go in and see the bears, Dolly and Loulou approached them curiously while Koda hid in the enclosure, eyeing them from a distance.

Debate will likely still continue about what caused the attacks, and the campers and the families and friends of victim Kevin Kammer and the injured Deb Freele and Ronald Singer will never forget that frightening night. Though it's been "civilized" by its many millions of visitors, Yellowstone is also home to wild, untamed animals that it protects by the mandate of its mission. Zoo Montana chose to give a home to the cubs that had been affected by the stresses on their environment, and in early January 2011, it was decided that rather than keep exposing the bears to crowds and more stress, they would give them a chance to hibernate for the winter before being exposed to visitors or being transferred to another zoo. After a man died in a mauling near Canyon Junction on July 2, 2011, park officials decided not to remove or destroy the bear—a mother with young cubs that had been surprised by the man and his wife as they hiked one day. Finding a balance that keeps the park safe and animals safe will always be a challenge.

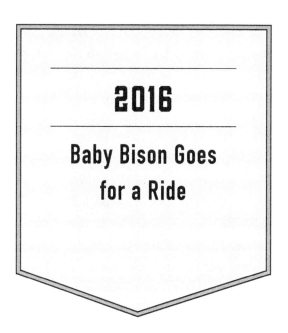

2016

Baby Bison Goes for a Ride

There are signs everywhere.

Yellowstone National Park is home to nearly six thousand individuals of the species *Bison bison*, with their giant shaggy heads, their comically undersized (compared to those giant heads) feet, and their potentially lethal horns. As you drive through the north gate at Gardiner, or in from Cody on the east, or through any of the other park entrances, you receive a famous yellow flyer headlined with the words "Think Safety, Act Safely: Yellowstone Is a Dangerous Place." On the flyer is a simple illustration, a human figure being flung into the air by a charging bison.

Along the nearly four hundred miles of roads in Yellowstone and at the trailheads for nearly one thousand miles of trails, visitors see simple, direct signs: "Danger:

Fragile Thermal Area Keep Out," "Dangerous Ground Boiling Water," "Animals Are Dangerous Never Approach or Feed," and, at regular intervals, a brown sign with the white silhouette of a large bison and the words: "Danger Do Not Approach Wildlife."

The signs don't work.

Every year, people wander off trail, trespass on restricted areas, and are waved away from close encounters with wildlife. Websites collect the tales of foolish behavior by tourists, and it seems that several times each year incidents make national news. In May 2016, one of the most infamous human-wildlife encounters unfolded in the Lamar Valley during the height of bison calving season.

Adult female bison generally give birth to their offspring between March and July each year. The newborns weigh between thirty to seventy pounds and are covered with reddish fur that will later darken to the rich brown of the adults, so they're easy to spot and provide endless delight for visitors who spot them with their herds at that time of year. After birth, the newborns, or "red dogs," as they are sometimes called, can keep up with their elders by the time they are two to three hours old—and they are well protected by the other animals in their herds, including their mothers.

At any time of year, "Bison Jams" are a common occurrence on Yellowstone roads, as the parade of campers, cars, and SUVs make their slow crawl around the grand loop with their eyes fixed on the landscape, searching out the wolves, coyotes, bears, elk, and bison who call the Greater Yellowstone Ecosystem their home. From simple cell-phone cameras to giant zoom lenses, visitors are found training their recording devices on every movement, hoping to catch that magic moment.

In May 2016, a woman named Karen Richardson was helping with a fifth-grade field trip to the Lamar Buffalo Ranch, when an SUV pulled into the ranger station with a red dog in its cargo area. The father and son who were driving the car insisted on speaking with a ranger, claiming that they had rescued the baby, which was struggling to keep up and shivering from the cold.

Bison, and especially the calves, look relatively harmless as they lumber across prairie and pick their way step by step across the roadways. They are somehow familiar-looking creatures that don't inspire fear and concern from their human observers. Bison are the cause of more injuries to visitors than any other animal. They're found all over the park, they're enormous horned beasts, and they can run at speeds of up to thirty-five miles per hour. They can swim, they can spin themselves around quickly, and they are not meant to be approached. The law says that people should not approach within twenty-five yards of the giant ungulates.

When the father and son from Quebec, Shamash Kassam and Shakeel Kassam, arrived at the Lamar Buffalo Ranch that day, they had a tale of a much-closer encounter that they would relate later to various news sources after Ms. Richardson's photo and the whole story went viral. They told reporters in Canada, their home country, that they had stopped to watch the animals and were told by another visitor that this particular "red dog" had struggled to cross a river and was shivering violently and leaning against a warm vehicle on the verge of collapse. The two men drove away but turned back to find the bison alone and made the decision to try to get help.

When a 911 call failed due to lack of signal, the men did what they thought was best for the small animal. The man later recalled, "I picked him up by the belly and put him in the SUV, in the back."

Once the pair reached the ranger station with their animal cargo, it became quickly clear to them that their act of kindness was not appreciated by park officials. They were immediately told that what they had done was against park regulations, unsafe, and dangerous for both them and the animal. Shamash Kassam was fined and directed to show the rangers where they had picked up the bison, and Kassam would eventually be charged for his actions.

After pleading guilty, Kassam would offer justification for his actions, explaining that when he lived near a wild-animal preserve in Africa, animals thought to be in distress were often taken to authorities for intervention. But in Yellowstone, it's hard to deny those signs and rules that are explained every few hundred feet down the road.

In the case of the baby bison, no humans were injured despite all of the warnings of what might happen to them if they approach these wild animals too closely. And despite the stories of tourists trying to photograph their toddlers atop the furry backs of these giants or just going in for a closer look and a pat of that remarkable fur, the thermal features of the park are still responsible for more injuries every year than wildlife—though, again, obeying those signs could help alleviate some of those injuries.

But the bison, which might or might not have survived its struggle in the wild, didn't have the choice to follow a sign and wasn't as lucky.

After rangers identified the location where the bison was picked up by the Kassams, they tried in vain to get it to be accepted by its herd. Unfortunately, the well-meant kindness turned out to be quite harmful when the animal had to be euthanized because it wasn't rejoining its herd and was causing dangerous interactions on the road.

The park service would later make this statement: "Interference by people can cause mothers to reject their offspring. In this case, park rangers tried repeatedly to reunite the newborn bison calf with the herd. These efforts failed. The bison calf was later euthanized because it was abandoned and causing a dangerous situation by continually approaching people and cars along the roadway."

Sometimes it's a little thing that leads to a very big adventure.

With more than 1,100 miles of trails, Yellowstone is a very big landscape for adventure, and hikers, backpackers, and campers take advantage of that every year. For some visitors to the Greater Yellowstone Ecosystem, heading out with a lightweight tent and backpack and a sturdy pair of boots, after getting the required permits, is the preferred way of investigating the backcountry. And some take advantage of the outfitters who provide their services and the services of horses, ponies, mules, burros—and llamas—to carry their gear and water and provide for their comfort and the ultimate backcountry experience.

Beau and Kristin Baty of Wilderness Ridge Trail Llamas had been providing those services for adventurers for about

eight years by July 2018, and they had led their string of llamas into the park for a once-in-a-lifetime adventure for their
guests. Among the llamas was a crafty older animal named
Ike.

In Yellowstone National Park, llamas, horses, and other
pack animals are allowed on park trails after July 1, and visitors to the area plan for these "trips of a lifetime" sometimes
for years in advance. The chance to see wildlife at a safe
distance but away from the crowded roadways and to hike
the trails away from the busy boardwalks is appealing but
doesn't come easy. Backpacking—bringing everything you
need for an overnight or longer trip with you in your pack—is
challenging and fun and made much easier when your gear is
hauled by pack animals.

Native to South America, llamas have been used as pack
animals for centuries. They have the ability to haul more than
three hundred pounds, they're smaller and more maneuverable
than horses, and they are also very territorial—they are very
effective at warding off predators, making loud alarm sounds
when predators approach and making chase or spitting.

In the case of the Batys that hot July summer, in their
string was a middle-aged—about twelve-year-old—llama that
had been suffering from a small thing that was about to lead
to a big adventure.

The Batys already knew that Ike was wily. He had managed to slip out of his halter on previous trips, but he had
been easy enough to catch those times. Now, though, the little problem that had been bothering him had added cranki-
ness to his wily ways. Ike had a toothache, and abscess, that
the Batys had been trying to treat, but his halter was aggravat-
ing it. The tooth problem was probably caused by a broken

tooth from a kick from another llama, and it had been plaguing Ike for a while.

In July 2018, in Yellowstone National Park, his pain pushed him over the edge. He slipped off the harness that was rubbing against his jaw and took off into the park alone and free. The Batys weren't able to retrieve him, and he did not come back to join his herd.

The rest of the summer, people spotted Ike. They'd be watching bison from their minivans or SUVs, and a white furry head would pop out of the trees and trot across the road. The toothache that had propelled Ike to leave his pack train made him extra territorial and antsy about human contact, but he never strayed too far from the roads and waterways inhabited by people and livestock. Based on the confirmed sightings over the next three months, his eventual rescuers could estimate that he was lurking in the woods and by the streams near some of the most popular places in the park.

But no one could catch up with Ike.

In October, the park was getting ready to transition to winter operations. Fewer entrances would be open and fewer tourists would be on the roads and on the trails. And the brutal winter weather of the Yellowstone basin was lurking in the near future and evident in the frosty mornings. Snow would come soon, forage would be scarcer, and the odds of Ike making it through the winter, all alone and still dealing with an infected tooth, were getting longer. Deep snow, wolves, and other predators would make Ike's winter especially dangerous.

A woman named Susi Sinay-Hülsemeyer, who owned a llama packing business near Pray, Montana, had been thinking about poor Ike since she'd first learned of his plight. Knowing that his last known location had been Lewis Lake, near the south entrance, she gathered four friends and three llamas from her own herd—unfamiliar to Ike—and headed into the park.

Unloading at a trailhead near the lake, the little band hiked into the woods. After about a mile, they still hadn't spotted him, but then his distinctive brown-and-white fur streaked by in the trees. He had spotted them—and had come running up to the other llamas.

Wary of approaching their human companions, he trailed along behind the furry pack train as they turned and made their way back to the trailhead and the trailers. Even though he wouldn't allow her to get too close, Susi could see the sore on his cheek and was determined to get him care as soon as they could.

The story of Ike the llama had made national news by the time of the rescue, and Ike's former owners, glad to hear of his survival but happy enough to have him in a new home, relinquished his ownership to Susi, who promptly renamed him Lewis in honor of the place where he was found.

Lewis's pain was diagnosed, and a plan was made for his treatment—but it would cost a whopping three thousand dollars to take him to Colorado to have surgery. The community rallied around the intrepid explorer, rallying behind Susi's GoFundMe in July 2019 after a Bozeman, Montana, TV station featured a story on Lewis and his adventures. Susi would take Lewis to Colorado State University for a major surgery—and he has now healed completely.

2022

Washed Away

Every year, more than three million visitors roll into Yellowstone National Park from all over the world. You can find places to visit in the park year-round, but when all entrances are open starting in April, it means peak travel, and that means crowds at Old Faithful, Mammoth Hot Springs, the Grand Canyon of the Yellowstone, and in the gateway towns of West Yellowstone, Montana; Cody, Wyoming; Cooke City, Montana; Red Lodge, Montana; and Gardiner, Montana. Tourism drives much of the economy in the remote corner of Idaho, Montana, and Wyoming that the Greater Yellowstone Ecosystem covers, bringing an estimated $600 million to the economy of the region each year. The small gateway communities, and even the larger nearby cities, see a big boost every year from dollars spent on hotels, food, and entertainment when visitors flock to the world's first national park.

The little town of Gardiner, Montana, on the Gardner River, is hardly ever a sleepy small town. Found right on the north edge of the park and home to the Roosevelt Arch and the official North Entrance to Yellowstone, its full-time population is just under eight hundred—the high school is small enough that they play six-man football, not eleven- or even eight-man. Hotels, restaurants, bookstores, and gift shops make up the bulk of the businesses in the town tucked between the mountains and the river—the closest town of any size, Livingston, Montana, is a little more than a half hour to the north, longer than that in bad winter conditions.

In the winter, hardy snowshoers, snowmobilers, cross-country skiers, and wildlife watchers still make their way into the park, through Mammoth Hot Springs. In the offseason, they can cross the Lamar Valley, keeping an eye out for the wolves that inhabit the area year-round and watching the bison break the crust of the snow with their giant shaggy heads. Snow, in the winter of 2021–2022, was at the heart of what was to come for the citizens of Gardiner—and the rest of Yellowstone—that spring.

Visitors can find snow in Yellowstone in any month of the year. At the higher but still accessible elevations, such as the road to Mount Washburn, it rarely melts away completely. Photos of happy tourists making snowballs and wearing shorts and sunglasses are part of summer in the park. Parts of the park get more snow than others—and the annual snowfall across the region is generally around 150 inches, or over twelve feet. Weather is unpredictable, though, and while parts of the park are warming, climate change has also meant that some winters are snowier and colder than others. Such was the case in the winter of 2021–2022. The snow fell and fell and fell, and then it didn't melt right away. When it did melt, it had to go somewhere. And then it started to rain.

Part of the appeal of Gardiner, Montana, in addition to its lovely downtown frontage overlooking the North Entrance to Yellowstone and its charming hotels, bed-and-breakfasts, and restaurants—plus the many outfitters who take trips into the park every year—is its location right on the river. You can sit on the patio at the Iron Horse Bar and watch the stream of visitors crossing the bridge to head in and out of the park-frontage area, you can take advantage of the outfitters and raft the river, and you can even stay in a hotel room that sits right on the edge of the riverbank as you plan your adventures. The road into and out of Gardiner also sits at the edge of that cut—you can spot moose browsing in the bosky areas near the banks and see them cross the rushing water, breaking through with their long legs and powerful torsos while their antlers rise like majestic crowns above. Homes, businesses, roadways, parking lots, and even the Gardiner Airport sit close to the water's edge.

Yellowstone is so remote and has such unusual geography that it's important to note that there is one main road into Gardiner and one road into the park from Gardiner. Small streets and side roads head to even smaller settlements, like Jardine, Montana, but in the winter, residents stock up on supplies in case of heavy snowfall that might keep them from making a trip to Livingston or just up the road a bit farther to Bozeman. The trip through the Lamar Valley, across the park to Cooke City and Silver Gate and then beyond to Billings, Montana, is more than three hours—and snow might still be a complicating factor in making the trip. When summer comes, with its tourists, tourist dollars, and crowded streets and restaurants, residents still plan for the unexpected, and they definitely expect to have to wait for a table at the pizza place.

Yellowstone sits on a high plateau—the caldera rim is at about nine thousand feet above sea level. Water from snowmelt in the park has to go somewhere, and it generally flows downstream. When above-average snowfall starts to melt quickly in the summer months, a lot of water flows downstream. On about June 10, 2022, park officials and state officials knew there was a major flooding problem coming. An unprecedented amount of rainfall had compounded the effect of the snowmelt, and a five-hundred-year flood event was beginning.

In Red Lodge, Montana, just north of the park's northeast entrances, it was like the river had started flowing down the main streets. Homes and businesses were damaged, and residents brought in sandbags and emergency supplies. Power was knocked out in entire communities. In Billings, the wastewater facility was breached, and in Mammoth, in the national park, waste from the compromised sewage facility began flowing into the Gardner River. Over that weekend, as the waters rose and sanitation and power failed, the National Park Service began evacuating the park.

Park entrances were closed to incoming traffic, and over 10,000 visitors and 2,200 employees were located and urged to leave in an orderly manner. Mudslides caused roads to fail, and houses ordinarily well away from the waters' edge were swept away into the raging waters of the rivers. By June 14, when the State of Montana ordered a state of emergency, the park was essentially emptied, and the damage was being assessed. The worst and most obvious was the road between Mammoth and Gardiner. A 750-foot section had completely collapsed, cutting off access from the community to the national park and beyond, effectively closing the North Entrance of the park and cutting off the remaining park employees from services there. Engineers deemed it beyond repair.

Outfitters, hotel owners, and restaurant owners in Gardiner were devastated. They had neighbors who lost homes to the floodwaters. Visitors who had planned stays there that summer would be canceling their travel. River and pack trips and zipline tours would be refunded, employees who had been brought in for the summer season would be furloughed. In mid-July 2020, just after the park had opened to visitors with pandemic precautions in place, several beloved and legendary downtown businesses had been destroyed in a fire and were still in the process of being rebuilt and replaced. Finally, after two years of global pandemic, the area had been looking forward to a robust summer season. Now, the closure of the park due to the floods looked to be another setback for the town.

The summer of 2022 was a quiet one in Gardiner. Visitors still dipped their toes into the area, but daylong stays were rare, and longer drives to the other entrances deterred visitors. The park's other gateways were open for business, but Gardiner was cut off from it, and even their regular deliveries that would come over the park roads were delayed by the need to detour.

Recovery began quickly but moved slowly. By July 1, a temporary North Entrance road was opened, which allowed park employees to get to work. And a system was established that would allow some tourist groups to use the road during "travel windows." Ever resilient, the people of the area did what they could to keep their town afloat and hoped for the tourists to return.

In 2023, 2.5 million people would visit Yellowstone National Park, the second-highest recorded number in history. As of June 2024, the road known as "The Old Gardiner Road" has been reopened as the main entrance to Yellowstone from Gardiner, Montana. Travelers can pass through the historic Roosevelt Arch and drive up the steep incline to curve around the hill and see the vistas of Mammoth Hot Springs open up before them once more.

2024

Yellowstone of the Future

At 10:50 a.m. one winter morning in Yellowstone, a few people had wandered out toward the snow-covered boardwalk on a frigid January day. Their parkas, hats, and mittens make for a great photo op against the winter landscape. The stark-white snow shines brightly around the gray sinter cone between the dusky green trees. At plus or minus ten minutes from 11:13 a.m., the show will begin.

The winter travel season in Yellowstone just started a few weeks ago, and it will be many more weeks before the snow all but disappears and soft grasses and wildflowers begin their springtime display in Yellowstone National Park. Few visitors make their way to Old Faithful at this time of year, so the crowd is virtually nonexistent, a stark contrast to the thick ropes of visitors who spread themselves along the boardwalk in July and August. For most of the time, the only evidence of people are the brown-and-white park service sign and the footprints in the blanket of snow.

From hundreds of miles away, webcam viewers feel the anticipation in the air as the first gushes of hot water bubble ever so low out of the ground, and one can almost hear a collective sigh as the geyser appears to go quiet, but then the majestic column of water bursts upward with its billow of steam made larger by the cold-weather eruption. You can picture the crowd—some of whom may be seeing the geyser for the first time—measuring it against the trees and guessing at its height.

The Old Faithful WebCam, a new installation in 1999, and continually updated since then, is making it possible or people in Tokyo and Sydney, Australia, to watch it at the same time I know from experience that it's not the same as standing near it on a warm day with the ultimate rubber-neck crowd watching it burst or seeing it against the cold, gray background of early spring and late fall—but I'm still excited by the experience.

Children in Japan, Argentina, Australia, and everywhere around the world can now log on to the Yellowstone National Park website at www.nps.gov/yell/photosmultimedia/web cams.htm and watch the updated photos every thirty seconds to actually see the source of the myths that erupted in the earliest days of exploration in Yellowstone. Teachers can illustrate the magic of geothermal energy or drive home a point about conservation with the ultimate visual aid.

Since it was first photographed in early 1871, Old Faithful has been the enduring symbol of Yellowstone National Park. Its presence on the internet certainly furthers the park mandate, "For the Benefit and Enjoyment of the People," by making it available to even more people. In August 2010, a new visitor center also opened at Old Faithful—a gorgeous modern building that showcases the science and the history in a manner befitting this natural wonder. I can't wait to see it in person next time I'm there. For me, Old Faithful never gets old.

Yellowstone Facts and Trivia

Yellowstone National Park is larger than the states of Rhode Island and Delaware combined. While most of the park lies within the boundaries of the state of Wyoming, the western and northern edges are found in Idaho and Montana.

In the year 1872, when the park was established, there were three hundred visitors to the park. Prior to 1877, there were no more than five hundred in the park in any given year. Today, more than three million visitors enter Yellowstone annually. In 2010, a record-setting more than 3.64 million people visited the national park, 10 percent more than in 2009, which was also a record setter.

It is estimated that there are more than five hundred geysers and ten thousand hot springs, hot pools, and steam vents in the park—more than any other place in the world.

Yellowstone's name is derived from an Indian name for the fork of the Missouri that flows through its magnificent canyon. The Yellow Rock River became the Roche Jaune to the French and then the Yellowstone to the English and American hunters who trapped near there.

In its earliest days as a public attraction, Yellowstone was also called Wonderland or Geyserland.

The staff members at Yellowstone's concessions are familiarly referred to as "savages" by park personnel. More than 3,700 people from all over the world come to work in America's first national park every year in the hotels, restaurants, and other tourist services. There are more than eight hundred Park Service employees stationed in the park in summer; there are about half that number year-round.

By the 1890s, thousands of people were visiting the park every year (as opposed to millions today). When wagons or stages met on the roads, the occupants would yell out their home state or country to one another in a friendly variation of today's license plate game.

Volcanic eruptions in the Yellowstone area occurred 65 million years ago. There is evidence that the geysers and hot springs of the park remained active during the periods of geologic history marked by glaciers that covered the region.

On average, the Yellowstone Plateau is eight thousand feet above sea level.

Early sightseers traveled through the park in open carriages with forward-facing seats called Yellowstone Wagons. They carried nine to twelve passengers and were pulled by four horses each.

The U.S. Army was appointed to protect Yellowstone National Park from poachers and souvenir hunters in 1886; it was supposed to be a temporary assignment, but after four winters they built Fort Yellowstone for a more permanent home. Parts of the fort still exist at Mammoth Hot Springs. The army remained in the park until the formation of the National Park Service in 1916.

Cars were first allowed in Yellowstone National Park in 1915; eventually, they would revolutionize the way people saw Yellowstone.

Tower Fall was named in 1870 by the Washburn-Langford-Doane Expedition—one of the first to purposefully explore the park with the goal of cataloging its wonders. The party had agreed not to name Yellowstone's features after themselves, but often even the descriptive names they used had deeper meaning. One of the gentlemen along on the trip had a sweetheart named Miss Tower in the States; the name Minaret (Minnie Rhett) suggested by another explorer was rejected as being too transparent.

France, England, and Spain have all at various times throughout history laid claim to the land that is now Yellowstone National Park.

Isa Lake at Two-Ocean Plateau in Yellowstone is unique because it drains into both the Atlantic and the Pacific Oceans. Even more unique is that because of its configuration: the east side drains to the Pacific and the west to the Atlantic.

Electric Peak got its name because of the shock explorers A. C. Peale, Henry Gannett, and A. E. Brown received when they approached the summit during a thunderstorm on July 26, 1872. It was once thought to be the tallest mountain in the park; that honor actually goes to Eagle Peak at 11,358 feet. Electric is actually the sixth tallest at 10,992 feet in height.

By 1956, 98.7 percent of park visitors arrived by car and toured the park from the comfort of their automobiles.

The Grand Canyon of the Yellowstone River is about twenty-three miles long and 1,200 feet deep at its deepest point.

Lower Falls is the tallest waterfall in the park at 308 feet.

Lodgepole pine, so called because its long, straight trunk was used in Native American teepees, has special cones that will only release their seeds for germination when the cones are heated by fire. As a result, lodgepoles are among the first trees to grow in burned areas. About 80 percent of the park is covered by lodgepoles.

Yellowstone National Park is about one-quarter of a larger area with similar physical characteristics and habitats, known as the Greater Yellowstone Ecosystem.

In winter, cars can only enter Yellowstone National Park through its North Entrance at Gardiner, Montana. From there, they can go as far as Mammoth Hot Springs to the south and Cooke City, Montana, to the east. Snowmobiles and snowcoaches can travel on park roads through winter. And cross-country skis and snowshoes are always a great option for winter tourists.

Yellowstone's Lamar Valley, in the northeast part of the park, is the winter home of thousands of elk and hundreds of bison because of its relatively mild climate and good grazing. The large population of elk in the valley was one of the reasons that biologists chose it as a good place to release the reintroduced wolf in 1995.

When wolves kill elk, they also provide food for eagles, ravens, magpies, foxes, and grizzlies, which scavenge on the carcasses.

Crawfish Creek, which feeds Moose Falls near the southern entrance of the park, is actually inhabited by crawfish, which can live there due to the fact that the water is warmed by upstream thermal features.

Steamboat Geyser, in Norris Geyser Basin's Back Basin, is the tallest in the world, with eruptions three hundred to four hundred feet in height. It is extremely unpredictable and can go months or years without erupting at all.

Echinus Geyser in the Back Basin at Norris Geyser Basin is the largest known acid geyser in the world. The water is more acidic than vinegar!

A microorganism called *Thermus aquaticus* was discovered in a hot spring near Great Fountain Geyser along Firehole

Lake Drive in the 1960s. It is now used in medical diagnoses and in DNA screening.

More than five hundred tons of stone were used to complete the lobby fireplace in the historic Old Faithful Inn.

Bison are the largest animals in Yellowstone and can weigh up to two thousand pounds.

Summer populations of elk in Yellowstone are around thirty thousand, making for the largest concentration of elk in the world.

Pronghorn, sometimes called antelope, are Yellowstone's speediest animals. They can run at speeds up to sixty miles per hour.

From 1891, when the park hotels first opened the garbage dumps where bears gathered to feed, until 1973, when all of the dumps were closed and bears began to be acclimated to more natural food sources, one to 115 people were injured every year by bears when they came in close contact with the wild animals.

Warren Angus Ferris, a clerk with the American Fur Company, was the first true tourist to visit Yellowstone's thermal wonders. He convinced a trapper to take him there specifically to show him the rumored geysers and hot springs in 1834.

BIBLIOGRAPHY

Books

Blevins, Winfred. *Roadside History of Yellowstone National Park.* Missoula, MT: Mountain Press Publishing, Co, 1989.

Calabro, Marian. *Operation Grizzly Bear.* New York: Four Winds Press, 1989.

Christopherson, Edmund. *The Night the Mountain Fell: The Story of the Montana-Yellowstone Earthquake.* Missoula, MT: Yellowstone/Earthquake Books, 1960.

Craighead, Frank, Jr. *Track of the Grizzly.* San Francisco: Sierra Club Books, 1979.

Ferguson, Gary. *The Yellowstone Wolves: The First Year.* Helena, MT: Falcon Publishing, 1996.

Haines, Aubrey L. *The Yellowstone Story,* Vols I and II. Boulder, CO: Associated University Press, 1977.

Historic Yellowstone. Helena, MT: The Historical Society of Montana Press.

Hulsemey-Sinay, Susi. *Lewis the Yellowstone Llama: A Journey of Courage.* Helena, MT: Sweetgrass Books, 2022.

Josephy, Alvin M., Jr. *Chief Joseph's People and Their War*. The Yellowstone Association for Natural Science, History, and Education, 1964.

Kauffman, Polly Wells. *National Parks and the Woman's Voice, A History*. Albuquerque: University of New Mexico Press, 1996.

Mattes, Merrill J. *Colter's Hell and Jackson's Hole*. Yellowstone Library and Museum Association, 1962.

McHugh, Tom. *The Time of the Buffalo*. New York: Knopf, 1972.

Miller, Mark M. *Adventures in Yellowstone*. Guilford, CT: Two Dot, 2009.

Raftery, J. H. *A Miracle in Hotel Building: Being the Story of the Building of the New Canyon Hotel in Yellowstone National Park*. Yellowstone Park Hotel Company, 1911.

Schullery, Paul. *Yellowstone Bear Tales*. Lanham, MD: Roberts Rinehart Publishers, 2001.

Schullery, Paul, ed. *Old Yellowstone Days*. Boulder, CO: Associated University Press, 1979.

Smith, Douglas W., and Gary Ferguson. *Decade of the Wolf*. Guilford, CT: Lyons Press, 2005.

Topping, E. S. *The Chronicles of the Yellowstone*. St. Paul: Pioneer Press Company, 1883.

Walter, Dave. *Montana Campfire Tales*. Helena, MT: Falcon Publishing, 1996.

Whittlesey, Lee. *Yellowstone Place Names*. Helena: Montana Historical Society Press, 1988.

Whittlesey, Lee H. *Death in Yellowstone, Accidents and Foolhardiness in the First National Park*. Boulder, CO: Roberts Rinehart, 1995.

Wingate, George W. *Through the Yellowstone Park on Horseback*. New York: O. Judd Co., 1886.

Yellowstone on Fire! Billings, MT: The Billings Gazette, 1989.

Yellowstone: The Official Guide to Touring America's First National Park. The Yellowstone Association, 1997.

Newspapers

Billings Gazette

Helena Independent Record

Yellowstone Today: The Official Newspaper of Yellowstone National Park

Brochures

"Canyon, Mud Volcano, Fountain Paint Pot and Firehole Lake Drive, Old Faithful, West Thumb, Mammoth Hot Springs." Yellowstone Association Publications.

"Yellowstone Roads and Bridges: A Glimpse of the Past."

Websites

Big Horn Basin Media: mybighornbasin.com/600-million -contributed-to-local-economy-by-yellowstone-national -park-tourism.

Bozeman Daily Chronicle: bozemandailychronicle.com/news/ famous-llama-who-once-roamed-yellowstone-backcountry -needs-a-dentist/article_bef1a2ab-2098-5355-a310-9b7f33 507dbc.html.

Great Falls Tribune: www.greatfallstribune.com/story/ news/2020/07/15/fire-destroys-businesses-gardiner -yellowstone-gateway/5442642002/.

National Park Service: www.nps.gov/yell/index.htm.

Today's Veterinary Practice: todaysveterinarypractice.com/exotic -medicine/lewis-the-llama-undergoes-successful-dental-surgery -at-csu.

Travel + Leisure: www.travelandleisure.com/nps-yellowstone -wildlife-bison-visitor-warning-7563975.

INDEX

ordinaries, 33, 36
Owen, William O., 34, 36

P

Peale, A. C., 144
petrified trees, 15, 46
Phillips, Charles, 79, 80
photography, 41, 42, 43, 44
Pitcher, Major, 58
poaching, 46, 48, 51, 70, 74, 143
poisonous plants, 80
postcards, 42, 44, 64
Pray, Montana, 129
predators, extermination of, 104
Pritchett, George, 17
pronghorn, 104, 145

R

Radersburg, Montana, 26
ranger-naturalist program, 74, 76
Reamer, Robert, 63
Red Lodge, Montana, 106, 131
Richardson, Tom, 64
roads, 34, 37, 39, 40, 53, 55, 61, 66,
    98, 99, 116, 144
robbery, stagecoach, 65, 66, 67
Rock Creek campground, 86
Roosevelt Arch, ix, 60, 136
Roosevelt, Theodore, 57, 58, 59, 60
Rose Creek wolf pack, 105

S

sagebrushers, 62
savages, 142
Schwatka, Frederick, 42
Shaw & Powell, 62
Sheepeater Cliff, 7
Sheepeaters, 5, 6, 7, 8
Sheridan, Philip, 37
Sherman, General, 25, 26
Shoshone Indians, 6, 7

Silver Gate, 133
Sinclair, W. K., 34
Singer, Ronald, 118
Soda Butte Campground, 115, 117
Soda Butte wolf pack, 105
Spain, 143
Specimen Ridge, 15
stagecoach robbery, 65, 66, 67
Steamboat Geyser, 110, 111, 112, 145
steam vents, 142
Sublette, William, 10
Sylvan Pass Soldier Station, 69, 70

T

tall tales, 14, 15
Targhee National Forest, 98, 100
Thermus aquaticus, 145
tours, 61, 62, 63, 64
trappers, 5, 7, 9, 10, 11, 14, 15, 74, 88
trout fishing, 94, 95
Two-Ocean Plateau, 143

U

Uncle Tom's Trail, 64
Upper Geyser Basin, 35, 59, 63
U.S. Army, 14, 25, 27, 28, 46, 143
U.S. Army Bicycle Corps, 36

V

vandalism, 46
volcanic activity, 2, 142

W

Washburn-Langford-Doane
    Expedition, 18, 20, 22, 143
Wasson, Isabel Basset, 75
water hemlock, 80
Waters, E. C., 51, 52, 63
West Yellowstone, Montana, 84, 131
Wilderness Ridge Trail, 127
Wind River Reservation, 8

ABOUT THE AUTHOR

Erin H. Turner is a writer and editor with a degree in history and gender and women's studies from Grinnell College in Grinnell, Iowa. She has traveled extensively throughout the West and all over the United States—including all fifty states and forty national parks—not including monuments and battlefields. She is also the author of *It Happened in Northern California*, *More than Petticoats: Remarkable California Women*, and *It Happened on the Lewis and Clark Expedition* and has edited numerous books on the history of the West as well as writing Reading the West for *Big Sky Journal* for more than a decade and contributing to other publications. After three decades living in Helena, Montana, she now lives in central Pennsylvania with her husband, Ross Johnson, and their two daughters, Lizzie and Stella.

Explore More

GLOBE PEQUOT IS YOUR GUIDE to special places, focusing on local pride close to home and helping you discover new destinations to explore from coast to coast. We publish books about iconic people and places, tapping into regional interest, history, cooking and food culture, folklore and the paranormal – all the things that make each region unique. With more than 75 years in publishing, we strive to give you the most up-to-date, regional information by local experts.

Globe Pequot

Available wherever books are sold.
Orders can also be placed at www.GlobePequot.com,
by phone from 8:00 A.M. to 5:00 P.M. EST at 1-800-462-6420 ext. 3024,
or by email at orders@nbnbooks.com.